John Freeman joined the then well-known Bristol printing and packaging company E. S. & A. Robinson in 1953. He worked in their flexible packaging company Colodense until 1996. Colodense became wholly owned by British Cellophane of Bridgwater in the 1950s. From the production planning department, John transferred to internal export sales in 1956. Eventually as the Middle East started to use oil wealth to develop its own industries, John started travelling regularly to the area in 1974 and continued to do so until his retirement.

LEAVING ON A JET PLANE

JOHN FREEMAN

FOREWORD BY ROBERT BOURNS
CHAIR OF TRUSTEES, ST PETER'S HOSPICE

SilverWood

Published by SilverWood Books 2012
www.silverwoodbooks.co.uk

Copyright © John Freeman 2012

ISBN 978-1-78132-034-1

British Library Cataloguing in Publication Data
A CIP catalogue record for this book is available from the British Library

Set in Sabon by SilverWood Books
Printed on responsibly sourced paper

This book is dedicated to Ve, a wonderful wife, mother, grandmother and a good friend to many people

All royalties from the sale of this book will be donated to St Peter's Hospice in Bristol

Foreword

On July 31ˢᵗ 2006 John's wife, Ve, sadly passed away – at home. John and his family were naturally devastated but relieved that Ve was no longer suffering and had been able to stay at home.

This was entirely due to the care and support she had received during the last twelve months of her life from one of the St Peter's Community Nurses, Jane Tyson. Jane cooperating with their GP was able to help Ve maintain a quality of life which at one time seemed unthinkable.

John and the family accepted an invitation from St Peter's Hospice to set up a Tribute Fund in Ve's memory to support the work of the Community Nurses and in the last six years have raised over £10000 and continue to fund raise in a variety of ways. John is donating all royalties from the sale of this book to St Peter's Hospice.

St Peter's Hospice has been providing real care and support to patients, their partners and families for 35 years. The clinicians and other staff working with the Hospice have developed expertise and are dedicated to ensuring that their skill and care are accessible to as many as possible in the community that we serve. We do so through the work of the In Patient Unit, the Day Hospice and increasingly by Hospice at Home. We work with our colleagues in the Health Service and other carers, sharing knowledge and expertise through the important work of our teaching unit.

The work is valuable and needed and relies on the

support of the community, volunteers and fundraisers. We are grateful to them all and particularly to John for so generously donating the royalties from this book. Thank you.

Robert Bourns
Chair of Trustees, St Peter's Hospice

Map of the Middle East

Chapter 1

Leaving on a Jet Plane

Dear Reader,

Do you like people watching? When you are at a bus stop or on a station platform waiting for a train, do you wonder what the people around you are up to? They may be also wondering the same about you!

Airports offer an even greater range of possibilities. If you have ever departed from Heathrow, then not only have you been in one of the world's busiest airports, arguably the busiest, but you have been part of the most varied group of people anywhere in the United Kingdom. 67 million people a year pass through the five terminals travelling to 170 destinations on 90 airlines.

With three hours check in time before departure, being the norm these days, there is plenty of time to look around you at the people who are also travelling. Some will be going on holiday or are tourists returning to their own country. Perhaps there are families saying goodbye to loved ones who live abroad.

Many different nationalities and races, all trying to find the appropriate check-in desk, and then the correct gate for their flight. In this organised chaos, the loudspeaker announcements and the rattle of the departure boards, all add to the frenetic atmosphere and the nervous anticipation of the, would-be, passengers.

It's not unusual to see groups of people, perhaps tourists, or a business delegation. The latter group will not have to face the hassle that the ordinary traveller faces. They will be guided through check-in and security without any fuss to a business class lounge, and served with coffee etc. They will be met at their final destination by embassy or consular officials and will quickly complete all the entry formalities.

Whilst you are waiting your turn in the check-in queue, you may look around at other check-in desks and observe a lone businessman. His suitcase is somewhat battered, with foreign hotel stickers and custom clearance labels attached. His briefcase is not the normal type, but a pilot style rectangular case, which just conforms to the airline's overhead locker regulations. If it is wintertime you may see that he is not carrying a coat, which would suggest he is travelling to warmer climes. Not for him is the luxury of special treatment. His company will be expecting a rapid return on their investment in sending him to far off markets.

The phrase "export or die" has often been used by politicians in their message to British industry at times of economic instability such as the one we find ourselves in now. The wise companies will have already been exporting for many years and will have incorporated it into their overall marketing strategy. Success in selling overseas takes a long time to achieve and requires the build up of trust on both sides.

So, my story covers my experiences in the world of exporting, eventually working in far off places around the world most of which were well away from the tourist trail.

I am not famous or a "celeb". I have not been kidnapped,

nor escaped death by inches. Neither am I a politician or ex-MI.6! I was just an ordinary export sales rep. working for a good British company.

I don't claim to have done anything that hundreds of other representatives haven't done, but nevertheless hope you enjoy my tale about my work, the places I visited, and some of the wonderful people I had the pleasure of meeting and working with.

OK. We are through check-in and security and have found the right departure gate. Now on board, ready for take off, fasten your seat belt, and listen to the safety instructions. It's going to be quite a bumpy ride.

Chapter 2

Everything must have a beginning

16TH CENTURY SAYING

September 1953, and Britain had entered a new Elizabethan Age. A young Queen had been crowned just three months earlier. The country was only just recovering from the aftermath of the Second World War, but the accession of the new Queen had given a new impetus to the nation. The first ascent of Everest by Edmund Hillary and Sherpa Tensing had thrilled the world when news came through on the eve of the Coronation.

All this was against a background of the Korean War coming to an end, only after two million people had died. The "Cold War" was to get even colder as the West's relationships with Russia became worse. Winston Churchill was Prime Minister at the age of eighty.

I was eighteen, and had moved to Bristol from Halifax when my parents relocated. My plan for the next five years was clearly set out. Three years at Bristol University would be followed by two years National Service.

My "A" levels had been taken at the Grammar School in Hipperholme, a village, near Halifax in the West Riding of Yorkshire. The school, founded in 1648, motto *Doctrina Fortior Armis* [Learning more powerful than weapons] prided itself on its record of getting its students to Oxford or Cambridge. It encouraged the parents of pupils to opt for arts-based subjects, including Latin, which at that time was a pre-requisite for getting into Oxford or Cambridge. This was particularly the case when choosing which subjects to study at "A" level. In addition to Latin, I had taken French and English Literature.

I am the first to admit that I was not the most focussed of students and did just enough to get by. I found too many distractions such as tennis, cricket, football, badminton, and a penchant for billiards at the men's institute in the village. All of this did not bode well and my form marks clearly indicated that I was not Oxbridge material. As my parents were moving to Bristol, I applied for a place at Bristol University and was accepted subject to passing the "A" levels.

I received the good news that I, somehow, had passed in the three subjects. I arrived in Bristol in optimistic mood. However, a nasty shock came when, a few days later, I received a letter from Bristol University informing me that they were unable to confirm my place as my pass marks were below the standard that they required. This was a blow and totally unexpected as no mention had been made of pass grades when my application was made.

I did not relish the idea of re-sitting the exams. My schooldays had not been the happiest days of my life, and I had been only too glad to leave school.

I decided that there was nothing for it but to bring forward my two years of National Service. I sent in the appropriate forms, and a couple of weeks later I was called for a medical at a centre in Bristol. About a dozen of us were shown into a room and told to strip off. There, stark naked, we were measured, weighed, and prodded in certain delicate places, and then told to get dressed and wait for an interview as to which branch of the services would have the pleasure of our company. When my turn came, I was told immediately that I was not going to be accepted for military service. I asked why not, but was refused an answer. I was given a form with a classification to the effect that I would only be called up in a time of national emergency.

So, in the space of a month, my whole future had been wrecked. I just could not understand this latest rejection. With all the sport I played, and the miles that I cycled, I was, I thought, very fit.

I went to see our doctor, who, after a thorough examination, could find nothing wrong. He said he would make enquiries on my behalf. This took him quite a while, but he persisted, and eventually was informed that my weight was a stone lighter than the normal weight for someone six feet tall. It was thought that I would not stand up to the rigours of army life.

There had been a number of high profile cases around the time of my examination, of men with certain disabilities being drafted into the army regardless of their condition. This had received much critical newspaper coverage and questions were raised in the House of Commons. Our doctor reckoned this was why I had been turned down, with the army medical people reacting to the widespread criticism and not taking any chances.

So I felt somewhat better about things, but what to do now? The next step was to find employment. I was realistic enough to know that my academic achievements plus an apparently suspect health problem, was not going to make my search easy. My English Literature "A" level might have got me a job in one of the city's libraries, and in fact I was offered a place, but it did not appeal at all. Latin wasn't likely to get me far. The Romans had left a long time ago! When I first started to learn Latin, some kind soul had written in my textbook:

Latin is a language, as dead as dead can be,
It killed the ancient Romans and now it's killing
me!

I did however enjoy Latin.

I thought my French "A" level could prove useful as Bristol had a thriving port and might offer some possibilities. Ships from around the world were guided by pilots up the river Avon under Brunel's Clifton Suspension Bridge and through locks, right into the heart of the city centre. The harbour was bordered by warehouses into which were loaded cargoes of bananas, sugar, wine, timber, tobacco, and many other goods.

I walked around the whole area noting down the addresses of all the companies and then sent letters to them all seeking an interview. Not one replied.

Meanwhile, I was scouring the situations vacant pages of the local newspaper. I did get a couple of interviews with Building Societies, which regarded me with great suspicion and said that I would need to study finance if I were to join them. More study did not appeal.

Getting desperate, I then struck lucky with two interviews on the same day. First I had an interview at the Bristol office of the R.A.C. They were looking for someone to deal with member's queries. After the usual questions, they offered me the job because they thought my northern accent would be reassuring to callers! So much for three "A" levels! The pay was £3 a week. I said that I would let them know the next day.

Later that same morning, I went to a printing factory. There a similar interview took place and I was set a simple maths test. They wanted someone to work in the production office. The job sounded a bit more challenging than the R.A.C. and it was for a normal five day week as opposed to the R.A.C.'s, which required weekend working. The pay was also £3 a week. I was offered the job subject to a medical and I accepted on the spot. The medical, later that afternoon, was completed without a problem, with their doctor too, puzzled by my National Service rejection.

I knew nothing about the company I was going to work for. I was just glad to get a job. Once I started, I discovered that the factory was one of several in the Bristol area owned by the Robinson family, who for many years had been amongst the most prominent of local industrialists along with the Wills and Fry families, all great benefactors to the city.

The E. S. & A. Robinson factories produced a variety of printed packaging materials. The original business had been started in 1844 by Elisha Robinson, when paper bags were made by hand and sold to local shopkeepers. In the 1850s, a machine was designed to make simple bags, and then a machine was imported from the USA, which could make bags of different shapes. Further developments took place and by the early 1900s over 800 people were being employed in the area producing products from paper and cardboard. Printing techniques were also advancing and being applied to the packaging.

The company I was working for was called Colodense, a name derived from 'dense colour'. The material being printed was "Cellophane" and special printing techniques had been devised to put opaque inks onto this transparent surface. The factory had only been open for twelve months and I then discovered that 50% of the business was owned by British Cellophane in Bridgwater. Anyone who has driven down the M5 or A38 in the years between the 1950s and the 1990s will undoubtedly have noticed the smell of bad eggs. This came from a chimney on the site extracting fumes from the manufacturing process. Many clever people had tried to find a solution to cure it, but never did. Strangely, local Bridgwater folk never noticed the smell!

The method of making Cellophane had been discovered in 1898 by three English chemists. However the commercial development of this innovative clear product was not started until 1935 when Courtaulds, in a joint venture with a French company, constructed a purpose built factory in Bridgwater.

It was not until after the Second World War that demand for this material really took off, and it was the Robinson family that recognised its true potential in printed form. A deal was done and initially production of Cellophane bags and wrappers was done in part of their existing paper bag manufacturing company.

Demand soon outstripped the ability to supply, so a joint venture was proposed on a 50/50 basis between E. S. & A. Robinson and British Cellophane. Licences to build new factories were hard to come by but, because of both companies good export records, permission was given by the Government and the Colodense factory opened in 1952.

So, by the time I started work in the production department, the factory was in full swing with twenty eight machines producing at peak times up to fifteen million bags a week. Other machines were producing printed Cellophane in roll form, and slitting and sheeting machines completed the production scene. This is only a small picture of what was happening, but I won't bore you with any more technical details.

For the next three years I was involved in all aspects of production planning. After the shock of the previous couple of months, I was determined to make a go of this opportunity and I made it my business to learn all about the different types of material and the ways to print them.

I got on well with all the folk who worked there. The company employed 250 people. My Yorkshire accent came in for a lot of good natured teasing, but the atmosphere was good and the company seemed to be at the forefront in its field, with innovations coming in all the time as technology improved.

It was one of these new innovations that gave me an opportunity, which was to lead to my introduction to the world of exporting.

Cellophane bags had always been sealed using adhesive. This often caused problems when the bags were put into boxes too tightly as the adhesive could be squeezed out and then stick to other bags.

A new bag-making machine had been developed in France, which sealed bags by heat and the company invested in two of them. They duly arrived on site and the engineers were keen to assemble them. However the instructions were, naturally enough, in French. The Company Secretary remembered my "A" level, and I was asked to work with the chief engineer to translate the manual. This took a couple of weeks, but we got there, and the new equipment was soon in operation. At last, perhaps my education was starting to pay off.

Not long afterwards, there was a major falling out between the Robinsons and British Cellophane, and as a result, British Cellophane took over complete ownership of the company.

Major changes took place as might be expected. One of these related to the way in which export orders were handled. Prior to the take over, all correspondence and finished goods had been channelled through the Robinson's head office. Now we were on our own. A director in London took over the export management and a correspondent was appointed in Bristol to work with him.

I was still working in the production department whilst these changes were taking place. After a couple of months, I was asked if I would transfer to the sales office to handle export enquiries. It appeared that the London director had a "short fuse" and had not got on well with the original choice. He had demanded a change. I didn't need asking twice and agreed, although it sounded as if I was entering the lions den!

Chapter 3

Not to advance is to go back
LATIN

So it was goodbye to my friends in production in one way, although I knew I would be relying on that friendship very soon. Relationships between sales and production were often frosty, as pressure on delivery schedules was frequent.

I thought that my geographic knowledge of the world was pretty good. My father's brother emigrated to Australia in 1926 and I had another uncle on my mother's side who emigrated to Canada in 1946. Like many boys in the 1940s, I collected foreign stamps. Small packets could be bought at Woolworths for a few pence and I tried to get stamps from every country in the world. I was fascinated by those countries that no longer existed such as Fiume, Heligoland, and Danzig.

Strangely, the subject of Geography was not considered very important in my school syllabus, and it was not taken to O level status. This disappointed me as it was the one subject which I actually enjoyed very much. We learned about the world in a variety of other ways. Empire Day was always celebrated. On the 24th May, or the date nearest to it if it fell on a weekend, the whole school would be assembled in the main hall to be addressed by the headmaster and some local dignitary. In our case it was usually Colonel Goldthorp D.S.O., who had served the country in two world wars and was a school governor. He would lecture us about the importance of the day.

Queen Victoria had ruled an empire, which covered almost a quarter of the universe. After her death in 1902, it was decided that children needed to be told once a year that they belonged, with others across the seas, to a glorious empire, and that the future of this empire depended on them. We were reminded about great British heroes such as Clive of India, General Wolfe of Quebec, and of course General Gordon of Khartoum. All very jingoistic stuff and it largely went over our heads.

The assembly always ended with the hymn:

Jesus shall reign where'er the sun
Doth his successive journeys run.
His kingdom stretch from shore to shore
Till moons shall wax and wane no more.

Written by Isaac Watts in the 1600s, we were growing up thinking that not only did Britain rule almost the whole world, but that world was either Christian or Heathen. Anyway, we sang lustily and gave Colonel Goldthorp three hearty cheers because we knew he would ask the headmaster to give us a half- day holiday.

Nowadays Empire Day has been consigned to history and is only remembered by people of my generation except, I understand, in Canada where it is officially recognised. Now our "empire" consists of a few islands dotted around the globe and Her Majesty the Queen presides over a Commonwealth of Nations.

The local vicar had been a missionary in Malaya, and regaled us boys with stories of head hunters who had regular battles with rival tribes and displayed trophy heads outside their dwellings.

A visit to the Wainwright Museum in Halifax left me feeling somewhat green about the gills after seeing a display of shrunken heads in glass jars.

So, I might have been quite good at knowing where in the world countries were, but my actual knowledge of them was, at best, fairly basic. We knew that the British Empire was those parts of a world map coloured red.

Looking back, I find it incredible that I had never seen a black man until one Saturday in 1950 a team turned up at Halifax Town with a black centre half. It caused quite a stir. I also recall around that time hitching a lift on the back of a lorry with some school mates to go and see McDonald Bailey who had represented Great Britain in the 1948 Olympic Games held in London. I think he was the only black athlete in our team and ran in the 100 and 200 metres. He was an amateur then of course, but after the Olympics joined St Helens Rugby League Club as a professional, and quickly gained a reputation as a wing three-quarter. We got into Odsal Stadium, the home of Bradford Northern, as did thousands of others, all anxious to see the great man. We were not disappointed and were amazed at his speed.

Any cinema films about foreign parts were usually adventures featuring Tarzan, Arab Sheiks, or the French Foreign Legion, none of which gave a true picture of the world, so I knew I was in for a steep learning curve.

The incumbent export correspondent was delighted to see me and couldn't wait to transfer to calmer waters. I had exactly one week to get myself up to speed. At least, by now, I had a good working knowledge of all the materials used and the different products that required them, so felt equipped to deal with most enquiries.

The Sales Office was located in the basement of the factory, about as far away from the Production Office as was possible. There, in the office, sales correspondents sat at their desks in a long line along one wall. Each correspondent was linked to a particular regional sales office and its representatives. Opposite each desk was another line of desks where the typists sat opposite the correspondent for whom they worked. Mine was called Joyce who was in her mid twenties. She was very helpful but not keen on doing re-types when her spelling let her down. This, of course, was long before the days of word processors, and there was a continuous noise of typewriters clicking away, rising to a crescendo late afternoon as the rush was on to meet the post collection deadline of 5pm.

I briefed myself quickly on Export terminology and practices. Quotations were required either FOB UK Port or CIF. The letters FOB stood for Free on Board, which meant that in addition to the ex-works price normally quoted, I had to add on charges for transport to the docks and loading on to a vessel. CIF took things a stage further. The cost of the goods, insurance and freight charges to the port of the country of final destination had to be calculated and added on.

Many clients required quotations in a particular currency such as the Dollar, Franc, or Deutschmark. No calculators in those days and fortunately, I had learned to use the slide rule when working out material quantities in the production office, so I had no problems here.

When sending out offers, we had to specify what payment terms we required. I had to work with the Chief Cashier who would take advice from our Bank depending on where the goods were going. Some countries were commercially sound, so open credit terms were acceptable. Others, however, required greater caution and we would ask for a Letter of Credit, which effectively meant that the client would deposit payment with a UK bank before production and we would draw payment after presenting shipping documents to the bank as proof of despatch. This however could and did cause frequent problems as the Letter of Credit often had a very tight final date specified. If production was delayed for any reason, we would have to file the documents late and we were then at the mercy of the bank to authorise payment. This usually worked out, but it could be a protracted business if the customer chose to be difficult.

I was learning all this as I went along. I found the London director, a man called John Forster, quite reasonable to get on with. He could be short tempered and I had a blast one morning after I had sent him an offer quoting Bulawayo as the destination port. Unfortunately it is some 400 miles inland!

At 8.45am each day he would ring with his instructions for the day. Telephone calls between London and Bristol had to be booked via a telephone operator. Cables would come in during the day from overseas customers or agents, delivered by Post Office motorcyclists on their red BSA Bantam motor bikes. Many cables were in a Bentley's code to save money, but of course I then had to refer to the code book to translate them. This system had been invented in the USA in 1919.

Mr. Forster was not far short of sixty-five and was due for retirement in the near future, so he was given an assistant in the London office. His name was Keith Shackleton, a grandson of Ernest Shackleton of Antarctic fame. However the two of them did not get on, which made things very difficult for me in Bristol. Soon I was in the middle of a tug of war between them. I would get an instruction from Shackleton only for it to be countermanded by Mr. Forster. The situation got worse and worse and only ended when Shackleton left suddenly, no doubt frustrated by the situation. It was a relief for me.

I don't know if it was the strain that he had been under, but a few weeks later Mr. Forster suffered a heart attack and very nearly died. London office was left unmanned, so I was told by our Sales Director to go and sort things out. No M4 then, so I caught the 8.15am "Bristolian" from Temple Meads station and arrived at Paddington at 10.00am precisely, followed by a short bus ride to Henrietta Street where our office was. There was a lot to do but I linked the mail to the relevant correspondence and brought the whole lot back to Bristol.

From then on, incoming mail was sent down overnight, and I had no trouble dealing with it. It was good practice. I did have to go to London several times to see the British Cellophane export team, who were in the same building.

It soon became obvious that Mr. Forster would not be able to return to work, even though he had recovered well, so the search began for a new export manager.

Our Sales Director was looking for a long term appointment. Several people applied but none were considered suitable. Quite suddenly he offered the position to the South of England area manager, Paul, who was 10 years older than me. Paul hadn't applied and was rather taken aback by the offer, but more or less accepted on the spot.

It was a few weeks before he could get involved, as a replacement had to be found to take over his area. In the meantime, British Cellophane was finalising its own export team and had appointed three representatives to travel the world. It was thought advisable for me to attend their briefings, as they undoubtedly would receive enquiries for printed material. The world had been divided into three sections – Asia, South America, and Middle East/Europe. They were planning on trips lasting up to one month, and would appoint agents in each of the countries visited. Our company was to use the same agents, which at the time seemed perfectly acceptable, but was to present me with problems many years later.

Paul and I hit it off straight away. He was a laid back character, ex-navy, married to Joan and had two small sons. He lived in Guildford and commuted to London daily. He was a keen hockey player but liked all sports, so we got on well. I made several trips to London to brief him on export procedure and made sure that I gave him the correct information to pass on to potential customers. If he brought clients to the factory, he always involved me in the visit.

Things have never stood still in the world of packaging. What you have to remember is that in the 1950s all shopping was done in small local stores. Messrs ForTES and COhen had not yet launched their superstores. Little pre-packed food existed as there was not the machinery to produce it. Cellophane was regarded as a luxury material, and paper was still "king".

Times were changing however, and companies making automatic packaging machines were beginning to make an impact. The machines weren't cheap, and could cost over £30,000 so, initially, it was only the major food companies who could afford them.

One of the first products to be switched to automatic packaging was the humble potato crisp. At that time the biggest producer was Smiths. Previously they had used a glassine paper bag, and older readers might remember the little blue sachet of salt inside each bag, which then had to be sealed by hand. A new production line which also applied salt or flavours, automatically fed crisps into a hopper, which then dispensed the correct weight into a bag formed by a packaging machine and sealed it. The packaging machine used Cellophane in reel form, and the printed design used a small rectangular mark on one edge which an electronic device picked up and triggered the sealing jaws ensuring that the design was always in the correct place.

Colodense employed two technical engineers to work with UK clients and the machine manufacturers, to sort out any running problems and in the early days there were plenty. Machine manufacturers were highly suspicious of the packaging material suppliers, and it took quite a while before mutual trust and co-operation was established. It didn't take long for many packaging machine manufacturers to come on the scene, and soon we were supplying material to be run on machines from Germany [east and west], Italy, Switzerland, and the USA.

Biscuits soon followed the way of crisps. Hitherto sold out of tins, machines were developed to produce packs such as those seen in supermarkets today. New types of Cellophane had to be developed to cope with these machines, and the rate of progress was quite staggering and took some keeping up with. More printing machinery was installed to meet the demand for reels, and this marked the gradual decline in the sale of ready-made bags.

My new boss, Paul, was settling in well in the London office, and I had no trouble working with him. Enquiries were now coming in at a rate from the agents, whom British Cellophane had appointed, and the number of orders gradually increased.

We had to be very careful when printing foreign languages.

Wording would be set in type and airmailed to the customer for checking. Our designers had to be aware of foreign culture too. Asked to design a coffee bag for a client in Kenya, the artist drew an elephant with its trunk hanging down only to be told that this was a sign of bad luck, and that the trunk should be up.

A customer in Trinidad, of Indian origin, got upset because a turban had been drawn, wound the wrong way.

The designers did have some success with a bakery in Honduras. The owner, a Mr Henry Ponting wanted his picture printed on his bags with him wearing a baker's hat. The artist managed to produce a very good likeness and Mr. Ponting was delighted with the result.

The 1950s came to an end with the company extremely busy. Export business was still considered as make-weight to the UK trade and it was often difficult to get it any priority. But gradually export turnover was starting to impact on company figures although there was a perception that it was not profitable, which was untrue.

Once Paul had settled in, he began to travel to meet the agents that British Cellophane had appointed. My work however remained largely the same, and I was beginning to feel marginalised.

Chapter 4

How poor are they that have not patience

OTHELLO WILLIAM SHAKESPEARE

From a work point of view little was to change for me. From the UK and world's viewpoint however, the 1960s were a decade of great change. In the UK, National Service ended in 1960 resulting in thousands of young men seeking employment, which often was not there, so causing social problems. South Africa witnessed the Sharpeville shootings, and the brutal implementation of apartheid. 1961 saw John Kennedy become President of the USA. A year later he was facing down President Krushchev of Russia over the Cuban missile crisis. Then the Berlin Wall was built. 1963 JFK is assassinated and the "Black Power" struggle led by Martin Luther King in the USA caused severe unrest.

The mid 1960s finds the UK economy in deep trouble, and Prime Minister Harold Wilson becomes locked in a long drawn out dispute with Ian Smith over the future of Rhodesia. Asia too was in turmoil. Although the Vietnam war had ended, India and Pakistan were at each others throats and the cultural revolution in China had been introduced to Mao Tse Tung's little red book. Spain also was trying to gain possession of Gibraltar, which the UK and Gibraltarians naturally opposed.

In 1967, when the UK trade gap was at its worst, the Labour government devalued the pound, and despite an "I'm backing Britain" campaign, it did little to help the economy. As a result, unemployment reached 500,000, and industrial unrest over the rising cost of living caused the government a real headache. Prime Minister Harold Wilson's promise that "the pound in your pocket" would retain its value soon sounded hollow. The end of the 1960s saw the IRA beginning its terrorist activities. Colonel Gaddafi took control of Libya, and the first men landed on the moon.

Trying to boost exports during this period became a priority for the country, but in a world where problems seemed to be cropping up all the time, it was a tricky business knowing where to try and develop markets that would remain stable enough to warrant attention. The UK joining the European Common Market in 1971 did not open any new markets for our company as there were many similar firms already established in the various member countries.

Paul was doing his best and had good markets in East and West Africa. He had taken on a fluent French speaking representative, Brian, to deal with the French territories in West Africa. I too had been given an assistant, Mike, to deal with the increased workload.

The 1960s for me had seen big changes in my own life. I had met and married a wonderful Bristol girl, Ve, and by the end of 1970 we had two sons and a daughter, so for me it was family life and their needs, that took priority over everything else, which is as it should be.

So, the challenge for UK businesses was to rise to the expectation of the British people of better things to come. All rationing had finished by the end of the 1950s and this had sparked a frenzy of activity in the food producing industries. Competition was fierce and colourful packaging soon became a marketing necessity.

At the same time, a generation was growing up that had not known the war years. Young people were developing their own culture and were frequently at odds with their parents.

Pre-packed food was still a long way off. People bought their fish and meat from their local fishmonger and butcher. These shops were in every high street as were grocers, greengrocers, bakers, and hardware shops. Competition among the major food producers increased, and the demand for our products grew so rapidly that delivery times were stretching out twelve to fourteen weeks, which did not please customers. As a result, there was a great deal of hard negotiating to be done with my former colleagues in the production office to maintain delivery dates when they were under great pressure from the UK sales people.

The weekly publication of Lloyds Shipping List required careful checking to find the closing and loading times of vessels. It required close liaison between our shipping clerk in the traffic department and the factory to meet the deadline. Despite a lot of hassle, the majority of shipments were made on time. Failure usually meant the added cost of having to use airfreight at our expense. As the export volume grew, the problems mounted, and my experience in dealing with them grew as well.

Paul and Brian were travelling more frequently. Trip schedules in the 1960s were tricky to organise because the availability of connecting flights was very limited. So trying to cover several countries on a trip often meant being stuck in one place longer than necessary.

Enquiries were now flooding in from East & West Africa, Bolivia, Peru, Caribbean, Greece to name but a few. The Greek connection was the result of a holiday taken there by our Sales Director. He had come across a small printing company in Athens. He decided that it would be a good thing to co-operate with them by not only selling them technical know-how but to act as agents and promote our products, in particular, to the dried fruit producers. For some reason these producers always wanted their offers calculated in square metres and in Deutsche Marks, which took me a long time to work out.

The Sales Director hitherto had not taken an active interest in exporting, but his Greek venture prompted him to start getting involved. There were frequent Chamber of Commerce meetings in Bristol with an emphasis on exporting and he insisted that I accompany him to these meetings. I didn't find them particularly useful as they focussed on major works in the construction industry or arms trade. They were also quite boozy dos, and I suspected I was being used as a chauffeur because, by now, I had bought an old Ford car, not what a Sales Director is used to! No company car for me!

Costs for quotations were prepared by hand in a dedicated estimating department. No computers or calculators were around then, and slide rules were used by all. Because enquiries came in by airmail, I had to try and get some priority given to the costing process in order to get offers back to customers as quickly as possible by airmail. However, with the best will in the world, it could be three to four weeks before a potential customer received a quotation for consideration. Imagine that in today's world.

However being stuck in the office whilst others were roaming the world was beginning to irritate and I really wanted to be more involved. But no opportunities presented themselves.

We did have some interesting visitors to Bristol. Rabindra Shrestha, was the owner of one of our most far-flung companies Nebico Confectionery of Kathmandu, Nepal. His designs were printed with the kukri, the curved dagger, which is the national

34

symbol of Nepal. After a tour of the factory he asked to be taken to Marks and Spencer's store in Bristol. There we spent a long time whilst he bought children's and ladies clothes to take back to Nepal. He had been given a long list by his wife!

One day I took a Polish visitor to lunch in Bristol. Poland then was under a harsh Communist regime. My visitor was the buyer for the State pharmaceutical company. As we walked through one of Bristol's main streets, a fire engine came thundering through with its siren blaring. My visitor, whose name I've forgotten, flung himself into a shop doorway as the fire engine passed by. He was clearly terrified and then extremely embarrassed as he explained to me that the sirens resembled those of the secret police vehicles in Warsaw, which everyone was in fear of.

Any travelling which I did was limited to the UK. For a while I made several visits to Heathrow, not to get on a plane, as I would like to have done, but to visit various airline offices. It all started when Air India, then called Tata Airways, wanted a Cellophane bag in which to put a sandwich for their in-flight meals. Our designers put various Indian landmarks on the bag such as the Taj Mahal. It was followed by orders for bags in which cutlery was placed and finally for a narrow bag for businessmen to put their fountain pens in whilst on the flight, because, apparently, pens had a tendency to leak at altitude.

This innovation was picked up by other airlines, and soon I was visiting Kuwait Airways, Iran Air, and South African Airways to supply similar products.

There was plenty for me to do but that unfulfilled feeling was growing stronger. Paul knew about my "itchy feet" and sent me to Jersey in the Channel Islands to set up an agency.

A new "wonder" material was now becoming available. It was polythene, a by-product from the petro chemical industry. It was cheaper and stronger than Cellophane and opened up a whole new range of end uses. For Jersey it was the potato growers who wanted it.

Strictly speaking of course, The Channel Islands could hardly be called an export territory. However, our Sales Director decided it didn't fit into any of the "home" areas so it must be "export" Through the Chamber of Commerce we had located a possible agent and I was to check the company out. If I was satisfied, I was to sign an agreement with them.

Bristol then had a new small regional airport at Lulsgate, which, today, is now a much bigger international airport. The regional carrier was Cambrian Airways, a name that has now disappeared. The flight to St Helier was on a Thursday morning, and I was due to return the following evening.

The prospective agent's office seemed very efficient, and they had a branch in Guernsey so I had no hesitation in signing them up. There was however another task for me in Jersey, and that was to sort out what appeared to be a tricky problem reported to us by a customer. He had bought a small lot of Cellophane bags printed in red with the words CHANNEL ISLAND KNITWEAR. Beautiful white sweaters had been put in the bags and they had been displayed in their shop window. Unfortunately the red ink had permeated through the Cellophane and had transferred onto the sweaters. The customer was not happy and was demanding compensation. When I questioned the way in which the sweaters were made, I found that chemical bleach had been used in preparing the wool. It was this that had reacted with the ink. If we had known this from the outset we would have used a different type of Cellophane which would have had a barrier to prevent any contamination. I agreed to replace the bags but refused to accept the consequential loss for the sweaters. The incident taught me to be very aware of manufacturing processes in the future.

The return flight for Bristol, Cardiff, and Dublin, took off late afternoon on the Friday. The weather had taken a turn for the worse. It was raining and blowing a gale. The plane was full, and most of the passengers were Irish workers going home to Dublin. Quite a few had consumed large amounts of alcohol and were in boisterous mood as they took their seats. As we headed out over the English Channel the plane was buffeted about by the gale force winds and the turbulence was significant. The result, as I expect you have already guessed, was extensive use of sick bags, and I was very glad to be leaving the flight at Bristol.

For a while, before a new Sales Director handed it back to the UK sales force, the Channel Isles proved to be a useful market although with an active agent around I didn't get the chance to go back.

My next "foreign" trip was to Eire, which I suppose could correctly be described as an export market although it didn't feel like it! Paul had made many visits but was now so pre-occupied with more distant markets that I was asked to handle it. The biggest company there was Cadbury's and in particular their demand for printed cut wrappers for Dairy Flake. It seems incredible that forty years ago an army of girls wrapped this product by hand.

There was a direct sailing from Bristol to Dublin twice a week on Tuesdays and Fridays, and there was always pressure to get supplies on these vessels. Failure to do so meant airfreight. One of the things the factory had to be careful about was making sure that the inks, yellow, purple, and white were fully dry and all trace of odour removed before the sheeting and cutting process. If this did not happen, chocolate could become contaminated. The factory even set up a dedicated "odour" panel to test each printing.

The agency in Dublin consisted of a small paper goods wholesaler, which knew the Irish food processors. The Director of the company was a difficult man to please. When things were going well he could be charming, but if any difficulties arose, like a late delivery, he would leave his office and it was up to me to tell the customer the bad news. He would then complain to our Sales Director about my poor service. Two other employees however, made dealing with this market a pleasure on the whole. Miss McArthy was the office manager. Miss Mac, as she was called, was super efficient and woe-betide their sales representative Dick and even the Director if they upset her.

I made a couple of visits around the area with Dick in 1972. The first lasted three days. Dick picked me up from Dublin airport and we headed north-west to Balleybofey, a small village close to the border with Northern Ireland. Dick warned me that the area on both sides of the border was very republican minded and said that I should be careful in what I said. I decided to say as little as possible and watch and learn from Dick. I found that the Irish liked nothing better than the *craic* and watching Dick in action was a real education. The meetings would revolve around politics, family, and the weather with no mention of why we were there until much later. Then orders would be placed in a few minutes.

This was the normal pattern at all the companies we visited. There were several shirt manufacturers and bakeries. Dick was given a couple of shirts, which were classed as seconds, and the bakeries were more than generous. He was married with five children so every little helped.

Some six months later, I spent a whole week with him.

This time we headed south and finally covered the west coast. Again Dick picked me up from Dublin airport and, as we crossed through Dublin to reach the main road south, I was shocked to see small children poorly dressed running about on the pavements without shoes on. Some areas of Dublin seemed very poverty stricken.

Our first stop was at Waterford. Here was the second largest producer of porridge oats in the country and one of our best customers. I had met the owner before when he came to Bristol on his way to the Cheltenham Race Festival. I was made most welcome and needless to say Dick left with a good supply of porridge oats.

We reached Cork by late afternoon, and checked in at the Glenvera hotel, which was popular with commercial travellers. In the early evening they were exchanging samples of the products they were selling, but Dick had nothing to trade, so lost out. Then it was off to the pub next door. What with all the talking and singing, it seemed difficult for them to find time to drink, but by closing time the Guinness had had its effect and they were all singing Irish rebel songs very lustily. This was followed by the Irish National anthem, which I didn't recognise, but Dick dug me in the ribs to get me to stand up.

The next morning with Dick having a hangover, I drove, and we made our way to Kinsale where we had a customer who made candles, not any old candles but very decorative ones and special ones for use in churches. There, sitting in the sunshine outside the factory next to Kinsale harbour, we had a very pleasant meeting followed by sandwiches for lunch. Dick left with some candles.

Then it was on to Bandon where there was another producer of porridge oats. This was a smaller customer but what made the visit unusual was their office, which had never been updated since the early 1900s. The meeting followed the usual pattern and after politics, family, and the weather, we got the next order. Before leaving however, Dick went to one of the ancient filing cabinets, took out a chequebook, and wrote out the amount of an outstanding invoice. He then gave it to the buyer to sign, which he did without a murmur. Dick knew exactly where the chequebook was kept and I was to see this process repeated several times during the week.

The next two days we spent working our way up the west coast visiting sausage and bacon producers. We also went to a chicken processing factory and what I saw put me off eating chicken for a long time. It doesn't pay to think too much as to how our food is processed.

A visit to a textile mill at Foxford proved interesting. It was run, with one exception, entirely by nuns. The exception was the buyer, the only man on the premises. Their main outlet for their beautiful woven cloth was Shannon airport. Here transatlantic flights would stop to re-fuel before continuing to Europe and American passengers were good customers. However the coming of the new 707 Boeing airliners meant that a stop at Shannon was no longer necessary and they were going to have to find new outlets for their products. Such was the superb quality that I didn't think they would suffer too much. I did buy a skirt length for my wife.

On the final day we visited several bakeries on the way back to Dublin. Dick, already stocked up with bacon and sausages, added the Irish wholemeal barm brack loaves. On the quiet country roads we would often stop and pick up a turnip or a few potatoes that had fallen off a cart so that by the end of the week Dick's family was well provided for.

I learned a lot that week but after my return, Paul decided

it was taking up too much of my time and my assistant took over Eire.

One of Paul's new markets was Persia/Iran. A large company called Pars Industrial had opened in Teheran making sweets and snack foods. The company was owned by the Khosrowshahi family, and the head of the family was frequently to be found at his home in Hampstead, London. Paul went to Teheran and quickly formed a good relationship with the company and orders came in. The main product to be packed was a corn curl snack called Pofak. They had established distribution agencies up and down the Gulf region from Kuwait in the north to Oman in the south. The product was so popular that they had difficulty in keeping up with demand as it was the first snack food product in that market. For me it meant several trips to London to see Mr Khosrowshahi, but no visits to Teheran.

There were, however, signs that other Middle East countries, especially those which exported oil, were starting to develop their own industries and try to become more self-sufficient, improving the quality of life for their peoples. The Middle East taste buds for things sweet had not gone unnoticed in the UK. For instance, Burton's Biscuits were sending a container load of chocolate "Wagon Wheel" biscuits a week to Saudi Arabia, and other UK packs now had to include Arabic script.

We had also been dealing for a couple of years with the Iraq Date Board, which had an office in London. Each year around May, they ordered millions of printed wrappers, which had to be shipped out to Basrah at the end of August. These had to arrive in time to coincide with the date harvest, which started around the end of September. The orders were split into four sizes – 4oz, 6oz, 8oz, and 1lb. Several different designs were chosen such as Lion of Babylon, Camel, or Sinbad. Finished packs were then sent back to Europe in time for the Christmas trade.

It was because of this business that I came into contact with a Mr John Toby. He was a retired British Army Colonel who had served in North Africa during the Second World War and had become involved in the date trade there whilst on secondment to the United Nations Food Programme. He was now acting as an advisor to the Iraq Date Board and was required to inspect shipments when they arrived in the UK. Dates were prone to infestation. During the packing process, blocks were passed through a gas chamber but this process could be flawed, hence the need for inspection before the packs reached the shops.

These blocks of dates were mainly used in cooking as opposed to the traditional boxed dates, which came in from North Africa. They could be found in greengrocers throughout the UK around Christmas time. This trade attracted the attention of date growers on the other side of the Shatt Al Arab delta in Iran which was then called Persia. Through various shipping connections, a group of five growers contacted Mr Toby and asked for his help in marketing their dates. The Iraq Date Board was in effect a co-operative of several date growers but the growers from Khorramshahr would not join together despite Mr Toby's best efforts to persuade them otherwise. They did, however, agree to a joint meeting and I was asked to attend to advise on their packaging requirements.

This turned out to be quite a comic business. Mr Toby invited us all to his house in Arundel to sort things out, but instead of talking to them as a group, the five insisted on seeing me separately in another room. It was a long day. Each had their own agenda over quantity, price, and design and no one wanted the others to know what they had agreed. Furthermore there was an added complication in that they wanted to register their designs in the UK, which afterwards meant quite a few trips to the Patent Office then based in London.

It was while I was working with Mr Toby that I fell foul of the "demon drink". In my younger days, in the last two years at school, we boys were encouraged to help the village postmen with the Christmas deliveries. It proved to be a rewarding time. I already worked for the village post office by delivering telegrams after school, so knew the area well. I was assigned to work with the parcel delivery van. People were very pleased to receive parcels, especially when we got to a remote farm. In the spirit of Christmas we often got offered some cake and a drink. Like most young men I sampled beer – hated it, spirits seemed to destroy my vocal chords, but I did like the taste of sweet wine.

I had arranged to meet Mr Toby at his London club to finalise a few things. His club was the Naval and Military Club in St James Square. It is more popularly known as the In and Out Club because of the large signs on the pillars at the entrance directing members cars or taxis when they drive up to the Club.

Business completed, Mr Toby invited me to have lunch with him during which I had a glass [only one!] of red wine. I bade him farewell and started to walk along the road towards Piccadilly Circus to catch the tube back to Paddington. I became aware that my legs were not moving as they should and I was sweating profusely. How I got to the tube station and then to Paddington I do not know, but it was not until I was on the train and travelling back to Bristol, that I started to feel better. So concerned was I that I made an appointment to see my doctor. It was his opinion that I had had an allergic reaction to the wine, and his advice was to stay off it in future. This seemed a bit extreme at the time, but the experience had so unnerved me that I took his advice and have not taken alcohol since. I can't say I miss it and as you will see later my abstinence has given me something to smile about.

The early 1970s saw a big reorganisation in the company. The M4 had opened in 1966 so London was only a couple of hours away by road. Paul and Brian relocated to Bristol, which in one way was a good thing from a working point of view, but certainly affected my general position in the company. Travelling abroad seemed further off than ever.

On the February 15th 1971 Britain "went decimal". The conversion from Imperial to Metric measurements caused all sorts of difficulties in the UK market, but for the export business it made life easier as most countries already used the metric system.

Communication technology was also advancing rapidly. Telex systems were a massive improvement and companies throughout the world quickly embraced this new form of communication. A new office was erected next to our telephone exchange and two machines were installed. For quite a while however, making overseas connections could take a long time. This meant frequent re-dialling and our operators soon got fed up with this situation. There was nothing for it but for myself and my assistant Mike, to learn the process and do it ourselves. Likewise, incoming telexes were transferred to tapes and we had to use a special decoder to get the messages that they contained. The system rapidly got better and we frequently had conversations with customers on the machines very much like e-mail chats today. It all made a terrific difference to the way we worked and resulted in even more enquiries and subsequent orders. For me though, it meant I was more desk bound than ever.

Decimalisation had not improved the nation's economy, and in 1972, unemployment had reached one million. A strike by the miners, which started in January, lasted seven weeks. It almost brought the Heath government down. A 'state of emergency' was declared and the nation experienced many power cuts as power stations were forced to close because of a lack of coal. Even though we had joined the European Union, prospects for growth looked gloomy. The trouble in Northern Ireland culminated in the shootings in Londonderry and "Bloody Sunday", leaving the nation in shock.

In the wider world, President Nasser in Egypt was ousted from office in a coup led by Anwar Sadat. In Uganda, General Idi Amin carried out the ethnic cleansing of the country's Asian population, resulting in thousands fleeing to this country. In 1973 Egypt and Syria had a disastrous war with Israel, and with the Middle East once again in crisis, European countries, including the UK, went into panic mode as economies slumped even further. With 80% of the world's oil then coming from the Middle East, the outlook was extremely bleak.

Getting export business therefore was even more essential than ever, but with the world seemingly always in turmoil, where were the markets?

Nigeria and the former French colonies in West Africa were occupying much of Paul and Brian's time with slim pickings elsewhere. They were under great pressure to find new markets. Out of this somewhat depressing scenario, an opportunity occurred which was to change my situation completely, and it came about in a most unusual way.

Chapter 5

All is well that ends well
18TH CENTURY

1974 had started badly for everyone. The on-going oil crisis was further heightened by a "work to rule" by the coal miners, and stocks of coal were running so low as to prevent some power stations producing electricity. To try and keep some sort of industrial production going, the Conservative Government enforced a three-day working week in order to reduce electricity consumption and conserve coal stocks. The order came into force on January 1st and was to last until March 7th.

Not only was the three day working week hitting industry and the working population, but the Government had imposed a wage freeze against a backdrop of rising prices. The inevitable strikes followed, and the winter of discontent seemed to go on and on even after March.

Any export business was welcome and I know that some orders were taken at cost to ensure that when the factory was operating, there was work for them to do. Again Paul and Brian were under pressure to find and explore new markets. One of the countries Paul had found was Cyprus, and just as we were starting to get some decent business, the island was plunged into civil war.

I was asked to go to Amsterdam to sign up a company

that had offices in the Dutch West Indies. Leaving home at 5am one wet, dark February morning, I drove to Heathrow and caught the first flight out to Schipol. Fortunately the office was in central Amsterdam and only a short way from the airport bus terminal. The negotiations weren't difficult and I was able to sign an agency agreement. An afternoon flight back saw me home by the early evening. I could hardly say it was a real export experience and I knew very well that it would not be me going to the West Indies.

With the economic situation in 1974 being so bad, I had to count myself lucky that I had a secure job. Money was extremely tight. Mine was the only income. At that time, wives had not become "emancipated" as they called it and gone out to paid work to supplement their husband's pay. That day was not that far off though. My wife was running a toddler's playgroup with a friend in a local church hall. This, of course, was voluntary work and she wouldn't have dreamt of being paid for it. Nevertheless, here I was, approaching forty, in a steady job, but with no real opportunity to progress up the career ladder.

Summer came and the working week returned to normal. During that time we had obtained some orders from Yemen Arab Republic. We were aware from contacts in the packaging machine world, that a large factory was being constructed in the south of the country at Taiz.

The company was owned by the Hayel Saeed Anam family, which had moved from Aden when Yemen was divided in two, and a communist state formed in South Yemen. Somehow they had managed to transfer all their assets and set up this venture in Taiz, which was not all that far from the border with South Yemen.

The Yemen Arab Republic was now a separate State,

albeit none too stable at this time. The country had been ruled by an autocratic Imam until 1962, when he was overthrown by a military coup. A Republic was then declared. The Imam fled to neighbouring Saudi Arabia but his supporters fought against the new regime. The civil war carried on for seven years with neither side getting the upper hand. The Imam's supporters were backed by Saudi Arabia and the Republicans by Egypt. Then Saudi Arabia and Egypt agreed to withdraw support and following more fighting, the Republicans finally gained victory. There was a reconciliation between the two sides in 1970 and former supporters of the Imam were given some Government positions.

Similarly there were frequent border clashes with South Yemen until a treaty was signed in 1972 pledging both Yemens to work together towards eventual unity.

Against this uncertain background the Hayel Saeed Anam family had set up businesses not only in Taiz but also in Sanaa, the capital of North Yemen.

Paul had tried unsuccessfully to get to Yemen, which at that time could only be done via Saudi Arabia. However, flights had been cancelled and he had to go elsewhere.

The Yemenis recognised the difficulty of air transport and set up an office in London to deal with all their European suppliers, which is where I came in. They had bought two packaging machines from Germany to wrap their sweets.

The next time you unwrap a sweet, I would guess that it almost certainly has a twist on either end. If you were to measure the width of the paper or film, it would be somewhere between 80 and 90mm. This has been the traditional method used on machines since the 1930s.

The new machines from Germany were going to use film only 70mm wide making a saving of up to 20%. Sweets would be pillow wrapped with a heat-seal at either end instead of a twist.

We printed their design with an assortment of four colours, white, yellow, blue, and red. Reports soon came back to us that ink was coming off the Cellophane and blocking the heat sealing process. The whole consignment had been rejected with a bill of £49000 unpaid so it was a very serious matter.

Our two technical staff refused to go and investigate the complaint. Paul, with his previous track record of trying to get to the Yemen, wasn't keen either and in any case was committed to other markets. Having talked the matter over with my wife, I decided to volunteer to go and see if I could negotiate a settlement. Our Sales Director was not at all keen on the idea, but with no other options and the customer pressing for help, he reluctantly agreed. There was also the not so small matter of an unpaid bill of £49000.

I set about organising the trip. Taiz is a small town with a local airport, which could only be reached from either Sanaa the Capital, or Jeddah in Saudi Arabia. The route via Jeddah seemed the best option so visas were requested from both countries. Vaccinations against cholera, smallpox and typhoid were required and my doctor also prescribed Streptotriad tablets to combat any stomach problems, and Septrin tablets in case of a water infection.

I don't claim to be the most practical of people, but I felt if I could understand the principles of the wrapping machine and the nature of the ink system, then I might be able to do something. I spent a lot of time with our chief chemist getting details of the melt temperature points of the four colours supplied. The technical people also showed me the layout of the German machine on which the material was being used.

They also gave me a pyrometer so that I could independently monitor the machine temperatures. This small metal box had a dial and two electrodes. Imagine what airport security would make of that today!

We had a contact in Jeddah with another biscuit factory, and it was agreed that I would go and see them on my return journey. They also agreed to meet me and book a hotel room, as I would have to stay overnight in Jeddah before going on to Taiz the next day.

So, on November 1st 1974, as Saudia Boeing 707 Flight SV 784 roared down the runway at Heathrow bound for Jeddah, I little realised how eventful the next seven days were going to be. All my pre-trip arrangements had gone according to plan. The only hint of anything going wrong was that only the day before departure, the travel agency told me that my flight departure time had been put back one hour. As there was no telex service to Saudi Arabia at that time, I sent a cable to my contact in Jeddah advising him of this change.

At Heathrow that morning, security had been very tight. A series of high-jackings had caused all airlines to tighten their procedures and I did have to explain what the pyrometer was when it showed up on the luggage x-ray machine. In addition to walking through the screening gate, all passengers were subject to a physical body search before boarding. It soon became clear why we had all undergone such high security when a Saudi Arabian delegation boarded and were shown into the first-class seats. With a prayer to Allah being intoned over the intercom, we took off, half-an-hour late, first stop Paris.

We had left at 11.45am and Paris was just 45 minutes away. More passengers joined the flight and after an hour on the ground we were off this time, non-stop to Jeddah. We were due to arrive at 11.30pm local time, three hours ahead of GMT.

Saudi Airlines, of course, do not serve any alcoholic drinks on board. In fact no airline is allowed to serve alcohol whilst in Saudi airspace. The new French passengers had found a way round this. We had taken on an additional air hostess at Paris, and as she came sedately down the aisle, I could hear a clinking of glass and from under her cape she produced some bottles of wine which the French passengers had persuaded her to bring on board. The Saudi stewards simply turned a blind eye and the wine was all consumed long before we entered Saudi airspace, but I did wonder what they did with the empty bottles!

From Paris we flew towards the Swiss Alps at 37,000ft with a cruising speed of 500mph. Over Geneva the clouds began to clear below us and we had a magnificent view of the Alps. Then it was over Italy following the coastline south and it was just getting dark as we left the "toe" of Italy and headed south east into the Mediterranean night.

The half-hour delay at the start of the flight was made up and we arrived at Jeddah slightly ahead of time. We were not allowed to disembark until the Saudi delegation had left the aircraft. Through the window I could see a fleet of large black cars and a heavy military escort so they must have been important or even members of the royal family. As I got to the exit door, the heat and humidity hit me. At nearly midnight, the outside temperature was 27c.

A large green bus took passengers to the airport terminal building and we were ushered towards passport control. Here, after a lengthy queue, my passport was stamped but taken away as my visa was a transit one. The official told me that I would get it back the next day when I left for Taiz.

Although I was a little concerned at being separated from this vital document, no warning bells rang which was probably as well in the light of what was to happen.

There was no green channel at the Customs desk and all passengers luggage was being checked. My English newspaper was confiscated which I found annoying. Having finally reached the arrivals hall, I looked around for whoever was going to meet me but found no one. I found out later that the cable I had sent did not arrive until the following day, after I had left.

I hadn't a clue where I was supposed to be staying and by now it was 1o'clock in the morning. Nearby, I heard English voices arguing furiously with an Arab who was telling them that their hotel accommodation had been taken over by the Saudi government as there was an oil conference taking place. I heard him say he had found somewhere else for them to stay, so I asked if I could join them. The men were from British Aerospace and very kindly agreed. We all piled into a small minibus and were taken to a hotel on the outskirts of Jeddah where a few Riyals persuaded a rather sleepy manager to open up a small annex across the road from the main building. It was now 2am.

My flight to Taiz was at 9.20am whilst the other men's flight to Riyadh was due at 6.30am so none of us were going to get much sleep. I fell asleep quickly but was up and about by 7.00am and was not due at the airport until 8.20am, one hour before departure. However a few minutes later there was a knock on my door. It was one of the men I'd met the night before. He told me that their flight had been brought forward by one hour without warning and they had missed it. He advised me to check my flight. I rang the Yemen Airways office and sure enough the flight had been brought forward one hour to 8.20am. I had not unpacked so grabbed my case and managed to get a taxi getting to the airport just in time to check in. Recovering my passport back out of the immigration office threatened to leave me stranded. Fortunately I had noticed that on my arrival passports were being put in a steel cabinet behind the official. Because time was pressing, he allowed me to search for it myself as it had a brown leather cover on it, which made it fairly easy to locate.

There were only a few people on the Yemen Airways Boeing 737, its one and only jet plane at that time. I was the only foreigner. The flight took us south down the Red Sea coast and then turned inland through high mountains towards Taiz. I could not help noticing that the landscape was very barren but that there were some cultivated terraced areas stretching up the mountain sides and houses that appeared to be built into the mountain and looked pretty inaccessible.

We disembarked at the small airport and walked across the tarmac to the arrivals building. The locals walked straight through. My passport was duly stamped but I was told to report to the police and register within twenty four hours. Welcome to Yemen!

The airport was about six miles outside Taiz. No one was there to meet me, but there were a couple of taxis waiting. I showed the driver a letter heading of the company and he nodded that he knew where it was. I had some Yemen Riyals and he probably charged me twice as much as for a local but off we went at high speed, horn blaring every few seconds. The road was not paved so that there were clouds of dust everywhere not only from our taxi but vehicles coming in the opposite direction. I recalled the prayer to Allah on the Saudi flight and trusted that the driver knew where he was going.

The time was almost noon when I got to the office

in central Taiz, and it was about to close. Apparently they worked from 7am to 12noon, and then from 4pm to 7pm. There was no sign of a factory. They arranged a car to take me to a hotel, the Al Ikhwa. This was perched on top of a hill overlooking the city, which was dominated on the other side of the valley by the Jabal Sabir mountain rising to 10,000ft. Taiz itself is 4,600ft above sea level and at that time had a population of around 100,000 making it the country's second largest city.

I checked in the Al Ikhwa. It appeared to be quite a new building and I was told that it had only been open for 12 months and had been used for a government conference earlier in the year. Air conditioning was provided by fans, which didn't have much effect, so windows were open. These provided entry and exit for small geckos, which were chasing flies.

I was glad of the chance to have a breather and take stock. It had been a hectic start to the trip, but after an hours rest, I went out onto the balcony of the hotel to take a look at my surroundings. Looking down, I could see that the old part of Taiz was encompassed by a high city wall dating back to the 13th century. Within this area were a mixture of flat top buildings seemingly crammed in together with one road visible, running through the middle of the city, exiting west and east. The buildings looked pretty ancient, and indeed the history of Taiz can be traced back to the 6th century when it was the original capital of Yemen. Traditional brown bricks were and are used to create a unique style of architecture. On the older buildings, windows were outlined in white.

Against this brown background, the white minarets of the mosques really stood out, especially the Ashrafiyah mosque.

Looking away from the old city, more modern buildings

spread out along the valley. The spectacular Jabal Sabir mountain, however dominated the whole scene. Looking at it closely I could see houses at various points which seemed to be clinging to the sheer rocky surfaces rather like limpets at the seaside. I was told that there were villages at the top of the mountain and people, mainly women, walked down the mountain to the city market every day to sell firewood or produce. This was a six hour walk down and eight hours back up. I found the whole dramatic picture quite breathtaking.

A car came to collect me at 4o'clock and took me to the company office in the centre. Someone took my passport and went to the police to get my exit visa whilst we discussed the plans for the next day. There was a big shock awaiting me when the man came back. Although the exit visa was not a problem, it was found that I did not have an entry visa to get back to Saudi Arabia. The Saudi embassy in London had made a mistake and had only given me one entry and one exit visa, which of course I had already used on the way to Taiz. The only way back to the UK was through Saudi Arabia. So now, as well as having a problem at the factory, I had to find a way of getting home. "Don't panic Mr Mainwaring."

It had taken the best part of three weeks to get the Saudi visa from their London embassy and now I had to somehow get one in three days if I was to catch my return flight to London from Jeddah.

Taiz did not have any consular facilities, so I was told that I would have to get to Sanaa and persuade the Saudi consulate there to help me. Fortunately the Hayel Saeed Anam Company had an office in Sanaa, and they agreed to contact the consulate next day to prepare the ground for my visit. Day two had certainly been eventful to put it mildly and I hadn't even got to the factory yet. With the visa problem to sort out, this only left me one day to try and settle the complaint.

I awoke with a start from a deep sleep. It was still dark as I switched on the bedroom lamp. The time was 4.15am. The sound, which had woken me, can only be described as a wailing siren. I opened the window and the noise, which had woken me, was twice as loud as it echoed off the Jabal Sabir mountain. I doubted that anyone could sleep through that!

This was the city's Muezzins calling the faithful to the first of five prayer times in the day. The call beginning with *Allah ou Akbar* "God is Great", was coming from the top of the minarets and lasted for around 15 minutes. As each mosque seemed to be competing with its neighbour, the call wasn't exactly tuneful! Whatever the vocal interpretation, the call throughout the world of Islam is the same.

Allah is the greatest.
I bear witness that there is no god but Allah.
I bear witness that Muhammad is the messenger
of Allah
Come fast to prayer.
Come fast to the success.
Allah is the greatest.
There is no god but Allah.

The city was certainly coming to life. Dogs were barking and the goats, which wandered around the street, were bleating. The goats acted as street cleaners, munching their way through all the rubbish that had been left outside. Men, getting ready for work, were revving their motorcycles, so no more sleep for me.

A car came to collect me and took me to the office just before 7am. I said I wanted to get to the factory as soon as possible as I knew that my time was going to be limited. I was not feeling too optimistic about the outcome. The factory was ten miles outside Taiz. An industrial area was being created and land had been allocated for this use. Just before I left the office, a call came through from Sanaa to say that if I could get to Sanaa by 10.30am the next day, Monday, the Saudi consulate would issue a visa in time for me to catch a flight from Sanaa to Jeddah on Tuesday. The office manager said he would arrange a taxi for me so now it was up to me to sort things out in the factory. No pressure then!

The route took us out from the old part of the city through a gate in the city wall. I noticed that all the men wore a curved dagger in the belt around their waist and they looked a pretty fearsome bunch. We followed the same dusty road out towards the airport and past it into desert scrub land. A few half-completed buildings were dotted along the unpaved road, and when we reached the factory compound it was the only completed building around. On the approach it looked like one of those French Foreign Legion forts, and I couldn't see the factory at all as it was surrounded by massive walls. There were two huge metal gates, which swung open as we arrived and I was more than a little alarmed to see guards carrying automatic weapons.

I met the factory manager, an Egyptian, Ali Khalil, who gave me a quick tour of the factory. He said the reason for the armed guards was that there was still some opposition amongst the nearby tribes to any signs of modernisation, and the factory had been subject to some attacks in the past.

The building was modern and air-conditioned which was just as well for the outside temperature was going to be 30°c at midday. The machinery was being operated by men along with dozens of girls who were all dressed in white traditional burkas and a head dress with only their eyes showing. I could feel their eyes following me as I walked around. The girls were collecting biscuits and putting them into boxes.

Then I was taken into the confectionery department where the problems lay. A reel of Cellophane was put into the wrapping machine and soon ran into difficulty as the ink started to come off a fouling the sealing jaws.

So started a very long process of me checking machine speeds, temperatures with the pyrometer, and regular cleaning of the heated jaws. I had brought with me several soft copper wire cleaning brushes. These were the sort that motoring or motor cycle enthusiasts will remember as being used to clean spark plugs. My brushes cleaned the jaws in no time much to the wonderment of the machine operator with whom I was working. His cleaning brush had very rigid bristles and was totally inadequate for the job.

I then noticed that the size of the sweets was quite small. In testing the four colours that we had supplied, I found that two had much lower melt points so I asked the operator to run these on the twist machine to see if the sweets would fit, which they did. The twist machine of course did not require heat so that was part of the problem solved. I then spent several hours experimenting with machine speeds and temperature settings using the pyrometer to check against machine readings. By late afternoon, I had established the optimum settings for the operator to use. The machine then ran for one hour with no problems at all.

Ali Khalil was satisfied with the result and said he would authorise the payment of the outstanding £49000. I was asked to send a good supply of wire brushes.

As I waited in Ali Khalil's office for a car to take me back to Taiz, an almighty thunderstorm broke out and for half-an-hour there was a torrential downpour. I was told that this phenomenon was a feature of this area and happened several times a week between 4 and 5pm.

I had also noticed during the day, an elderly man wandering around. He was dressed in white robes and headdress, and everyone treated him with the utmost respect. Ali Khalil told me that this was Hayel Saeed Anam, the head of the family. Although his sons ran the business, he liked to come in and see what was going on.

As I prepared to leave, Ali Khalil said he would like to see me during the evening. I was tired but obviously couldn't say no. The car splashed its way back to Taiz, but before going back to the Al Ikhwa, I called into the office to find out what the arrangements were for my journey to Sanaa. I was told that a taxi would pick me up at 4.45am. I hoped that my evening with Ali Khalil would not go on too long so I could get some sleep.

Ali Khalil picked me up at 7pm and he drove down the hill into the city, stopping at a nondescript building but which had the sign CASINO outside. I thought this very odd as gambling of any sort is not allowed in a Muslim country. We were shown into a room with a long table and chairs. Apart from the regulation photograph of the Yemeni President on the wall, there was no other decoration. Almost immediately, we were joined by several men, whom I recognised from the factory and the office. I was asked what I would like to drink and asked for a Coca Cola. The look of astonishment on Ali Khalil's face was clear to see and I had to explain to him that I kept off alcohol. Then it was my turn to be surprised when everybody else ordered beer. I then found out that whilst technically alcohol was banned, if they were entertaining a foreigner, then they were allowed to drink. No doubt this explained the gathering somewhat larger than I expected!

Conversation centred around family and politics and I thought back to my time in Eire. To my surprise also, Ali Khalil presented me with the traditional curved dagger in its decorated leather holster. It was the fearsome weapon that I had noticed all the Yemeni tribesmen wearing and I wondered how on earth I was going to get it back to the UK.

Around 8.30pm I could see it was getting dark outside and the gathering was preparing to leave. Ali Khalil told me that a curfew was due to come into place at 9pm so everyone wanted to be home by then. As he drove me back to the Al Ikhwa I noticed armed police being deployed at road junctions.

I didn't need my alarm clock to wake me up. The Muezzins saw to that. Amin, the taxi driver came at precisely 4.45am as promised. Fortunately he spoke reasonable English which was just as well as my Arabic was almost non-existent. He said we were going to take the direct route to Sanaa and he reckoned he could do it in five hours and would get me to the Saudi Consulate in plenty of time. Taking the direct route might sound like the blindingly obvious thing to do, but nothing in the Yemen was straightforward at that time anyway. The problem was that the direct route of 158 miles was still under construction. Although the route had been marked out and levelled, the German contractors had only got 60 miles south of Sanaa, so we would be travelling almost 100 miles on a dirt surface through two mountain ranges. The alternative route on a paved surface would go from Taiz to Hodeidah on the coast, and then inland to Sanaa, a total distance of 310 miles There was simply not enough time to use this safer route.

As we drove down into the city and through the streets, people were outside, some cooking a meal on paraffin stoves.

They looked very eerie in the light given off by the stove's flames as it was still dark. We avoided small groups of goats doing their morning cleaning round and the odd dog barking at us. Then it was out into the suburbs and here the paved road ended. The car's headlights weren't up to much. I guess the battery was always low due to excessive use of the horn.

We had not gone far when Amin suddenly braked hard. There was a large boulder in the middle of the road. It was too big for us to shift, but Amin just managed to squeeze around it. He said that it would have been put there during the night by the tribesmen opposed to the building of the road and indeed any modernisation, which brought the National Government in closer contact with them. The tribes jealously guarded their territory, and it was a sign that the conflict between the Republicans and the followers of the old Imam was far from over.

Amin was not keen to hang around, and rather agitated, he started to drive faster, too fast, because a few minutes later, going round a corner, we ran into a big pile of sand on the side of the road. No damage was done but the day wasn't going well for Amin. He reversed out and we drove on at a more sensible speed.

After an hour and a quarter without any further incident, we reached a range of mountains and started to climb higher and higher. It was now getting light and the sun clipping the tops of the mountains was a magnificent sight. Now it was light, I also noticed several skid marks near the unprotected edge on the left hand side of the "road". I was very glad that we were travelling on the right, hugging the inside route up the mountain.

A remarkable view greeted us as we reached the top of the mountain pass at the top of the Jabal Sumara, which must have been around 10,000ft. We stopped for a few minutes to admire the view. All the surrounding mountains were terraced going all the way up. On the plain below we were looking towards Ibb, which is known as "The Green City" surrounded by a patchwork of fertile fields and in the distance a further range of mountains.

I would have loved to have stopped and have a look around Ibb, but time was pressing. We covered the next thirty miles to the next mountain range in good time passing through the small town of Yarim, whose history dates back to the kingdoms of Saba, or perhaps better known as Sheba.

Another long ascent took us to the top of another pass, and it was here that poor Amin had another spot of bother. A green car shot past us and then stopped abruptly right in front of us causing Amin to slam on the brakes. The car driver got out and came back to our car. He opened Amin's door and pulled him out. There then started a furious argument with lots of shouting and arm waving. The green car's windscreen was splintered and it appeared that a stone, thrown up by our car's rear wheels, had hit the green car, which must have been travelling very close behind us. It was an accident, pure and simple, but Amin was getting the blame, and the situation looked to be getting out of hand. I thought I'd better give him some support so got out of the car and joined them. This seemed to calm things down, and the driver of the green car got back in and drove off much to our relief.

We reached Dhamar, roughly half way, and were glad to get to the paved road. Again there was no time to have a look at the town. As we drove through I saw buildings that were different from those seen in Taiz. Dhamar is situated at around 8,000 ft above sea level in what was once a volcanic area and the houses were trimmed with black volcanic rock stone. Just outside Dhamar, we stopped just to give Amin a break. As we stood by the car a Yemini came by with his heavily laden camel. The man had a chat with Amin and was quite happy to pose for a photograph with the camel. I couldn't help noticing a can of Shell fuel on its load.

Now it was another descent onto a flat fertile plain passing by several villages all of which had a fort on higher ground, a reminder of the frequent fighting, which had taken place among the tribes in Yemen.

The road was now dead straight and disappeared into a dot in the distance. However, poor Amin's troubles were not over yet. We approached an army checkpoint. There had been several on the way especially on the mountain passes where a strategically positioned tank could command control of any approach by an enemy. So far we had not encountered any difficulty in passing through these checkpoints. A soldier would look through the window, and after a quick word with Amin presumably to verify my credentials, we were waved through. Here though as we were getting nearer to Sanaa, the road was blocked with oil drums. We were behind a big lorry, and as that was being cleared to proceed, a soldier indicated to Amin to go round the lorry. As he did so and accelerated, another soldier stepped out from in front of the lorry and was struck by the side of our car. He went sprawling onto the floor. I think his pride was hurt more than anything else, but for the second time that day, Amin was yanked out of the car and another argument started. This time I was more worried because the soldier was carrying a gun and looked well capable of using it. Once again I got out of the car and the sight of a foreigner seemed to do the trick. The soldier dusted himself down and went off muttering and waving his arms.

Finally we drove the last twenty miles and reached Sanaa

at 9.30am without further incident. What a journey!

My first impression of Sanaa was of a sprawling city contained on all sides by mountains. Traffic of all descriptions clogged the streets, cars, pick up trucks, motor bikes, donkeys, horses, and camels all jostled for position, and there seemed to be no rules, just every man for himself. The general chaos extended to traders with stalls on the verges, and shops with piles of goods stacked up in front, almost toppling into the road. I hoped I would get the chance to explore.

From a tourist brochure, which I picked up in Taiz, I learnt that Sanaa is said to be one of the oldest cities in the world and one of the highest capitals at 7,500ft. Some historians say that its history goes back to the time of Noah's son Shem. Whilst this is disputed by other experts, the region can be traced back 2,500 years to the rulers of Sheba and of course to the Queen of Sheba who famously searched out King Solomon. It tells something of the wealth of the region at that time when you read about the gifts that were taken to impress King Solomon. The journey to Jerusalem, must have taken many days, and the long camel train carried 4,000 kilos of gold and large quantities of jewels and spices.

As in Taiz, the architecture was very distinctive and many buildings were multi storey and decorated with different coloured bricks or stone. In the old part of the city, some buildings were hundreds of years old. Mosques with their minarets were dotted around the skyline.

Amin threaded his way through the traffic mayhem with much use of the horn and we arrived at the Hayel Saeed Anam office. There was no time to waste. I bid farewell to Amin and thanked him profusely for getting me to Sanaa despite all the difficulties. I wondered what sort of journey he was going to have on his return to Taiz. The office manager took me to the

Saudi Consulate, and I handed in my passport together with the appropriate fee, just before the 10.30am deadline. I was told to come back to collect the visa at 4.30pm. Next we went to the Yemen Airlines office and rearranged my flight ticket.

A room had been booked for me at the Palace Hotel. This in fact had been the Palace of the old Imam, and was in the traditional Yemen architecture style. It was a lovely building and it's the only time I've ever slept in a room with stained glass windows.

After a couple of hour's rest, I decided to go on a walkabout. The market was nearby and all manner of goods were on sale, clothes, spices, fruits, ornaments, antiques all displayed on stalls. Above the general hustle and bustle, I could hear the sound of metal being hit and found a blacksmith's forge where the curved daggers were being made.

The next day, Tuesday, was a national holiday to celebrate the fourth anniversary of the revolution, which finally ended the rule of the old Imam. My flight wasn't until 1.30pm with a check-in-time of one hour before, so I took the opportunity to have another wander round the streets. The traders were out in force and no one seemed to mind my presence or my taking photographs. I could see why the Romans when they came to Yemen around 200BC called the area *Arabia Felix* – "Happy Arabia". This seems a far cry from the pictures today on our television screens as protests against the present regime take place with much loss of life both in Sanaa and Taiz.

I checked out from the Palace Hotel and took a taxi to Sanaa airport on the outskirts of the city. It was jam packed with Yemenis. It was the period in the Islamic calendar when Muslims go on the Haj pilgrimage to Mecca. It is everyone's desire to do this at least once in their lifetime and it is considered an honour to be able to include the word *Haji* in your name.

I knew therefore that my flight would be full and crowds had gathered on the rooftop observation area to wave their relatives off. As the inbound Yemen Airlines Boeing 737 touched down on the runway, a strange silence fell over those watching. It was quite eerie. Once again I was the only foreigner travelling, so I was kept back until all the Yemenis had boarded then allocated one of the crew's jump seats.

It was chaotic on board. The passengers were mainly male, all dressed in the traditional pilgrim's garb of white towelling. A couple of obviously very sick men had been loaded onto stretchers and placed across the seats at the back. I couldn't help wondering if this was a one way ticket to Mecca. I just hoped that they would make it.

As the flight took off, passengers ignored the pleas of the cabin crew and crowded to one side to try and get a glimpse of their relatives. I guess that for most, it was their first flight and for many, the first time that they had left their villages.

I felt sorry to be leaving this wonderful country, and wondered if I would get the opportunity to come back. There was so much more that I would like to see. All the people I had met had been most friendly and helpful.

It was mid afternoon when we arrived in Jeddah and the outside temperature was 35°c and 100% humidity. When my suitcase came along the belt, it looked decidedly the worse for wear. I had bought what I thought was a top quality suitcase from Boots in Bristol. Now it was gouged all across the top and one of the locks was hanging off. Then I noticed that the Yemeni luggage consisted almost entirely of large rectangular metal trunks and my suitcase had suffered as a result. Fortunately I had a strong strap with me so was able to secure the case.

Customs and immigration clearance took an age, and my

passport disappeared into the immigration official's cabinet once again. I made a mental note of which drawer it was in. I was relieved to find someone waiting for me, proof that a cable sent from Sanaa had arrived this time. I was taken to a hotel, and there, was able to take a shower and relax a bit. At least the room was air-conditioned.

As day turned into night, I decided to stretch my legs and explore the surrounding area. The Red Sea Palace, a grand title, but not living up to its name at that time, was in central Jeddah. The humidity had fallen, but it was still very hot. In the main street I passed an area used by the money changers. With pilgrims coming from all over the world, they needed somewhere to obtain Saudi currency. I was staggered to see piles of different currencies lying on top of tables, often without anyone there. Then I remembered that Saudi Arabia follows Sharia law and thieves can have fingers severed or hands cut off if caught. Friday was beheading day!

Next day, Wednesday, was spent in a new biscuit factory, part of which was still under construction. No attempt had been made to protect the baking lines from the dust that was being created on the building site. Brand new equipment was already dirty, and I was glad that I wasn't invited to sample any of the products. The chief baker was a British man and I was surprised that he wasn't taking more care over the plant hygiene. I commented on the dust but he merely shrugged his shoulders. He then said he would come and see me at the hotel that evening.

The owner then gave me details of the various packaging lines that he was looking for and said that initial orders were guaranteed, but would be compared with similar orders being supplied from Italy. Comparisons would be made on quality and price. I had the feeling though that the factory was so chaotic that doing business with these people would cause our company many problems. This feeling was confirmed when the British baker came to see me. He said that for a 5% commission he would file poor reports about our competitor's supplies and see to it that our material was always ordered.

This was the first but not the last time that I had such a proposition put to me. I tried not to show what I thought about this and told him that our company would not accept such a proposal under any circumstances.

The factory owner had invited me to his house for a meal that evening. I did wonder whether I should report the meeting I had had with his baker, but decided that it would be better to keep it to myself and see what happened after the first delivery of our material. I had also met a Syrian man at the factory who claimed that he had acted as an agent for our company and had introduced this new biscuit company to Colodense. He claimed he was entitled to a 5% commission as well. This was all getting a bit out of hand. I later discovered that this gentleman made a habit of attending European packaging exhibitions. He would then collect the catalogues of various companies and then wander around the Middle East claiming to represent them. I had to make it clear to the owner that we were not represented by him, and would not be paying him any commission.

A car picked me up from the Red Sea Palace at around 9pm and took me to the house where another European, a Swedish engineer, had also just arrived. We were shown into a room devoid of any furniture but with cushions all around the floor. I sat there with my Swedish friend wondering what was going to happen next. It was also his first experience of Arab hospitality so he couldn't tell me what to expect. Our host made fleeting appearances, and other Arab men gradually came in and took up positions sitting on the cushions. Sweet tea in little glass cups was served but there was no sign of any food.

Eventually, just after 11pm, we were each given a plate and a sharp knife. Two large plates of steaming rice were brought in followed by a whole roast lamb on a huge platter, which also contained all manner of salad dishes.

One by one, the others carved themselves a chunk of lamb and spooned a pile of rice and salad onto their plates. Everyone ate using their hands. We did the same but the Swede was getting nervous because he had heard that a sheep's eyeballs were considered a great delicacy and were offered to special guests. He wasn't at all keen on the idea and neither was I. We need not have worried for that honour went to a couple of the other men who, thank goodness, were far more important guests than us.

It was well after midnight when I was driven back to the hotel. Although tired, I couldn't get off to sleep. I sat reading a copy of Monday's Daily Telegraph, which I had spotted in the hotel shop. I saw the football results, Bristol Rovers 0 Southampton 1. I also noticed that any photographs showing any part of a woman's body had been covered in black ink, and any reference to Israel had received the same treatment. I had also bought a Middle East map and Israel had been blacked out on this too.

I did sleep eventually, but had to awake early as my flight back to the UK was at 10.15am. I had re-confirmed my booking with Saudia the day before, and the flight time was confirmed. However on arrival at Jeddah Airport, I found that the flight had been put back by three hours. It was no surprise that at passport control, the official said he couldn't find my passport. I told him which cabinet it was in, and sure enough, it was found. The scanner in security showed up my curved dagger. It was taken away and I was told to reclaim it when we reached Heathrow.

As we took off, I thought back to what an extraordinary seven days it had been. More by luck than good management I was going home on time. The problem that I had been sent to deal with had been solved to everyone's satisfaction. I had survived a punishing travel schedule and had seen some fabulous places and met some very interesting and pleasant people. Would I want to do it again? You bet I would! But what would the company say? I was not at all confident that they would give me the chance.

The flight followed the coast of the Red Sea northwards and we crossed over into Egypt following the Nile all the way up to its Delta. I could see green fields on either side of the river but they didn't extend outwards very far before the desert took over. Then it was across the Mediterranean to Italy, the Alps, France, the English Channel, and into Heathrow. Sure enough it was raining and cold.

I saw the long queues at Immigration and of course took advantage of the UK citizen's channel. I claimed my dagger from the Saudia desk without any problem. I then phoned home and spoke to my wife. This was the first contact I had been able to make in a week. How different things are nowadays. On the coach back to Bristol the green of the fields struck me in a way I had never noticed before.

Although it was a big relief to be home and share my experiences with my wife and the children, I wondered what the reaction was going to be at the office. I had learned so much in one week, and thought if I can cope with that, I can cope with anything.

After the weekend at home, I returned to the office on Monday, and filed my report. The technical people got my detailed figures taken in the hours spent on the problematic packaging machine. The Finance department told me that they had already received the £49,000 payment, so everyone was happy.

I was summoned to the Chairman's office. He was a Courtauld's appointee and was rarely seen about the offices. He had a reputation as a brilliant businessman, and had been appointed mainly to further the growing expansion of the Courtauld's Packaging Group by take-overs of existing companies in Europe. The Greek connection was already well established, and factories were now operating in France, Holland, and Spain. He was also involved, with my boss Paul, in setting up a factory in Nigeria.

I went into his office on the top floor. He was a heavy smoker of cigars and I could see him through a haze of smoke, peering at a world map on the office wall. Seeing me he said "where the ******* hell is the Yemen?" I pointed out where I had been on the map, and then had to sit down and tell him all about the place. It then transpired that he had a relative who had been offered a job in Jeddah and really just wanted to know some basic information about what life was like there and how much it cost. In this respect he was able to do one positive thing. The maximum daily allowance for overseas representatives at that time was £20. This was fine for Europe and Africa but had it not been for the fact that my hotel bills in the Yemen had been paid by the client, I could have been in trouble in Jeddah where even the most basic rooms were costing £90 a night. So in future, allowances were more realistic. I don't recall ever speaking to the Chairman again.

Chapter 6

Yet still we hug the dear deceit
NATHANIEL COTTON 1705-1788

My trip taught me several valuable lessons. The first was
not to rely totally on a travel agency to fix your itinerary
and documentation. The ABC Air Travel Guide is or was
published once a month. Although it was the size of a Yellow
Pages catalogue, with a little practice, it was easy to use
and then there's nobody to blame but yourself if you get it
wrong. Secondly check and double check all visa and hotel
bookings and get these confirmed in writing, and carry the
confirmation with you.

It did not feel however that I was going to get another
chance to put this gained knowledge to good use. Christmas
and the New Year breaks came and went. Paul and Brian
made their travel plans for 1975, and as far as I could see, I
would fall back into the old routine.

Then suddenly, one morning in February, I had a call
from a man in London. He said that there was an Iraqi
businessman coming to his office that afternoon, wanting to
place a large order for printed Cellophane. I got the OK to go
and see him and to cut a long story short, secured a big order.
What was more important, I started a long and successful
business association with a remarkable man, Abdul Wahab Al
Bunnia. He was an imposing figure in full Arab dress. He was

quite disfigured around the mouth, and shook hands with his left hand, as the right hand was somewhat deformed. I found out later that he had had an accident in a fire as a child.

During the meeting I discovered that not only did he have a large biscuit factory, but factories making sweets and chewing gum had also been built, all of which would need our packaging.

Shortly afterwards, we had a visit from the British Cellophane agent in Iraq, Leon Sarkis. He also represented our company, although to date this had not resulted in any activity. I told him about the transaction with the Bunnia company, and was told that this was by far the biggest in the private sector. More importantly Mr Sarkis confirmed that Iraq was embarking on a massive programme of industrial expansion to try and make the country self-sufficient particularly in all things relating to food. He said that someone should visit as soon as possible to survey the market.

Paul was in a quandary. He was very involved with the Nigerian project. Brian was about to leave to work with our Dutch company, and the new bilingual rep was still getting to grips with French West Africa.

I could see that this could be the opportunity I'd been waiting for, for so long. I talked it over with my wife Ve. As ever she was fully supportive and I would not have gone ahead unless she was. Paul knew I was itching to go, so went to the Sales Director to convince him that it was the right move.

I knew that Paul would have a job convincing the Sales Director. I didn't fit the image of a sales rep. For a start I was now approaching forty, whereas most of the UK sales force were in their twenties. I disliked the weekend sales conferences and never stayed overnight if I could possibly avoid it. Paul had similar views but, craftily, usually managed to be abroad when these events took place.

Paul managed to get reluctant approval and I set about organising what was to be the first of thirty seven visits to Iraq up until 1990. This took place in April 1975. Before I left, the Sales Director took it upon himself to give me a long lecture on selling techniques. Whilst I tried to look as interested as possible, I knew, even from my short time in Yemen and Saudi Arabia, that UK methods would have little or no relevance in the Middle East.

One of the things I had to get before I left, was a new suitcase. On my return from Yemen and Saudi Arabia, I took my battered case back to Boots to show them what their top quality product had suffered. It was a sorry sight and the manager was very taken aback. He gave me a full refund and kept the evidence to send back to head office. There was nothing else in their product range that I thought would stand up to the sort of conditions I had seen. I went to a specialist luggage shop in Bristol and explained my problem. The shop assistant was a very large lady and she showed me a "Globetrotter" case. This had a laminated exterior supported on the inside by a wooden frame. To prove its strength she jumped up and down on it several times, and I was convinced. It was expensive but fortunately the company reimbursed me. It was a good buy, and it lasted for nearly 10 years.

So it is Iraq that I have to thank for giving me the opportunity to show what I could do. So many bad things have been written about that country that I decided to give people a different perspective. My book *Iraq – From Adam to Saddam* tells of all my visits to this wonderful country. The people I met and worked with are the most generous and hospitable folk you could wish to meet. Iraq's culture and history are fascinating in their own right and after all, the cradle of civilisation itself can be found there.

For the people of Iraq, what started as a period of great prosperity in the mid 1970s, turned into a nightmare of dictatorship and repression during the next decade. I observed on each trip, after Saddam Hussein came to power, how his grip and that of his family and allies in the Baath Party, were affecting business and the lives of ordinary people. Gradually a climate of fear was everywhere and no criticism was ever made in case someone overheard the remark. I knew of at least two people who simply disappeared. One of my business contacts who was a member of one of Iraq's most prominent families, was killed by a bomb, which had been placed under his car.

The disastrous war with Iran from 1979 to 1988 virtually bankrupted the country and businesses closed. Then the crazy invasion of Kuwait in 1990 brought about a total humiliation of Saddam but not until he had done untold damage to Kuwait.

Quite why he was not chased all the way back to Baghdad is something I don't understand because it gave him time to recover and then, because of the needless sanctions imposed by the United Nations, he appeared to be the strong leader standing up against unwarranted foreign intervention.

So what had started so well in 1975 was well and truly over by 1990. Saddam Hussein brought shame and dishonour to a proud and historic country.

George W. Bush and Tony Blair carried on and just about destroyed Iraq. They may have got rid of a dictator, but what followed will surely be condemned as a crime against a people who had already suffered enough. I am sure that both men will go to their graves convinced that what they did was right. The Chilcot Enquiry will no doubt shed some light on this but I suspect that there are things, which will remain hidden, and the full truth will never be revealed.

Nathaniel Cotton, from whose writing I took my chapter heading, was an 18th century physician who specialised in mental health issues. He noted that people who had mental problems would cling to the most fanciful ideas and no amount of persuasion would make them think otherwise. This is what made them dangerous.

The chaos, which has enveloped Iraq since Saddam's removal, has led to horrific bloodshed on an unprecedented scale. This continued as 50,000 American troops stayed in Iraq albeit in a so-called non-combative role. Extremists, from all across the Arab world, continued to cause mayhem whilst they were there. Only now, with the withdrawal of all US forces, will Iraq have a chance to start recovering. The divide that has been created between Sunnis and Shias will take a very long time to heal and there are still extremist elements intent on keeping the unrest going.

Sunday May 22nd 2011 was the day that the final group of British military personnel left Umm Qasr, completing a withdrawal after eight years. This event received much coverage on the UK television news.

Sunday May 22nd 2011, sixteen civilians are killed when a suicide bomber struck in a crowded Baghdad market. Nothing about this incident appears on British television. Perhaps, because it was an all too regular occurrence. In May alone there had already been five such deadly attacks leaving many dead. Yet the British Foreign Minister, William Hague was reported as saying after the British withdrawal, that, "Iraq was a much better place than we found it". Try telling that to children without fathers, wives without husbands and families who have lost children, and all the relatives of the thousands upon thousands of Iraqis killed since President

Bush's "Mission Accomplished" statement.

I daresay that you have recognised my anger as to what happened to the Iraqi people. My anger is only directed at the politicians, not the military personnel who were sent there, many of whom lost their lives, or suffered terrible injuries too, like the people they had "liberated".

But this is not all. Thousands have fled Iraq, and taken up residence in Jordan because it was too dangerous for them to stay. One of these was my friend Moustafa. He became our company's agent when Leon Sarkis left Iraq in the early 1980s. He was an extremely effective agent and between us we established business with over sixty companies. His office was in central Baghdad and he was much respected by other businessmen. We kept in contact after 1990 right through to the outbreak of the second war, and then I lost touch. However I still wrote and sent cards but received no reply. I feared greatly for his and his family's safety when all the terrible events were taking place.

Then one day, out of the blue, two years ago, I had a telephone call from him. He had escaped to Jordan with his wife and son and they were now living with a relative of his wife's. His experience I suspect was typical of that which happened to many ordinary Iraqis trying to maintain some sort of business life. Central Baghdad had become just too dangerous to enter and his office could not have been more central. The main Post Office was closed, which was the reason why he never received my letters and cards. In an attempt to resurrect his business, he started working from his home, but this proved impractical. Then events in the suburbs of Baghdad took a very nasty turn. There were gangs of insurgents operating in Baghdad who kidnapped businessmen and held them to ransom for huge amounts. This happened to one of his neighbours and worse still, another was murdered. That was the final straw and Moustafa decided that it was just too unsafe to stay. Like many Iraqis before and after, he got into his car with his wife and son and drove to Amman. There he remains for the foreseeable future trying to do business. He will return to Baghdad one day but when is a big question. My letters and cards finally reached him courtesy of a friend when the Baghdad Post Office finally reopened.

Iraq and its people will recover one day. It will take a long time for old wounds to heal and it still has the potential to be the dominant economic force in the Middle East. Abdul Wahab Al Bunnia is still alive and the framework of all the companies he established is now under the supervision of his sons. They will set the standard that others will follow.

Chapter 7

From the Old to the New

Back to 1975 now. Before setting out for Iraq, my boss Paul thought that I should start to explore the possibility of doing business in Kuwait. We advertised for a local agent through the commercial section of the British Embassy and received what looked like a promising response from one company. I also wanted to go and meet the date packing companies in Khorramshahr, so I got an Iranian visa.

My flight from Baghdad was in the evening, so the approach to Kuwait was in darkness, but flames were clearly visible from the oil wells as they burnt off the gas.

Immigration was less complicated than for Iraq. I had an entry permit. Technically, because of a reciprocal agreement between the UK and Kuwait, a visa was not required, but I did need an entry permit. I could never work out the difference!

A taxi took me to the Sheraton Hotel in downtown Kuwait City. Hotel rooms were at a premium then, but my agent to be, knew the manager and had been able to get a room for me, for which I was very grateful.

Next morning I was taken to the office of Slaiman Esh Shaya. I could not help noticing on the way, that all buildings appeared to be new. There was no sign of anything ancient and I thought back twenty four hours when I had been visiting Babylon in Iraq. Moving from a country with thousands of years of history to a country with virtually no history was quite a culture shock to me. There were no old buses, battered cars, donkeys or pack horses. I couldn't see any narrow alleyways or old markets. Instead there were modern buildings, wide highways, and endless big American style cars.

Virtually all the buildings in Kuwait City have been built since 1961 when Kuwait became an independent state after being a British Protectorate. Kuwait's prosperity is founded purely and simply on its oil revenues. The link with Britain goes back to the end of the 19th century. The area then was a fairly barren land inhabited by wandering tribes. In 1899 Britain took control of the land as it was seen as a strategic position at the top of the Gulf and a link on the trade routes to India and the Far East. One of the major tribes was the Sabah family and it is they who then became rulers, but with Britain responsible for their foreign affairs. This treaty ran until 1961 when Kuwait became a fully sovereign state. The Sabah family set up a democratic parliament, one of the few in the region.

The total transfer of power in 1961 did not go without incident because shortly afterwards, Iraq lodged a territorial claim over Kuwait as it saw it as an opportunity to get a deep sea port. Oil had by now been discovered and protecting this tiny state became vitally important. British troops were despatched to Kuwait but were almost immediately withdrawn as troops from other Arab countries, alarmed by this aggressive act by Iraq, took over the role of protection. Faced with such overwhelming opposition, Iraq withdrew its claim. Shades of what was to come in 1990!

Oil revenue literally created a "rags to riches" scenario

and with a population of less than one million at that time, made it the richest per capita country in the world.

With so much wealth, many Kuwaitis employed non-Kuwaitis whether to run factories, or even the complete business. It was estimated that there were up to 300,000 educated Palestinians running most of the economy. Similarly there were thousands of Philippino and Sri Lankan men and women working as domestics and hotel staff, another complete contrast to Iraq.

Kuwait in the summer months is unbearably hot, and most affluent Kuwaitis leave for cooler climes. Beirut was a favourite before its troubled times. Greece too was a popular choice as was London and, shortly before my departure, I had met a Kuwaiti in London who complained to me that it had not rained enough!

Slaiman's office was fully air conditioned, and it felt like walking into a fridge after the heat outside. He was a tall striking figure, dressed in the traditional white dishdash and head dress. He told me that he was the youngest member of the Esh Shaya family and the family's main business was the importation and distribution of electrical goods of all descriptions. They also held several car dealerships.

Slaiman, however, had decided to follow a different line of business and was dealing in paper products designed for the food processing industry. He also had a contact in Dubai, which I knew could be important in the future. It seemed the ideal appointment and I said I would send him an agency agreement on my return to the UK.

There were two industrial areas, one by the port and the other near to the airport. At the port area we visited a flour mill making pasta. I found that there was little prospect of doing business as the owner had an Italian supplier who let him use a villa on the Italian coast during the summer. I didn't think the offer of a fortnight in a B & B in Weston-Super-Mare would be sufficient incentive to make him switch suppliers!

We had more success at the other industrial area near the airport. Here a new company was producing cakes and was owned by a friend of Slaiman's. I also met the bakery manager who was authorised to place orders. His name was Bernhard, of Swiss origin, but now based in London and a fanatical Arsenal supporter. I obtained our first orders and for once the product was worth eating.

Another interesting character was Mrs Waheeba. Our appointment was during the early evening. She was a large Egyptian lady who was employing girls to make potato crisps in her kitchen and she wanted Cellophane bags. It was a small order but nevertheless added to the range of printed samples that I could show prospective clients in the future. We were well entertained with tea and cakes.

Kuwait was never going to be a volume market like Iraq, but the business was worth having and what's more, could be done on open credit terms because of the country's financial standing.

On the two evenings I was in Kuwait, there were spectacular electric storms, and on the short flight across the Shatt Al Arab delta to Abadan, we flew through a severe storm causing major turbulence and a very bumpy ride.

On my first day in Abadan I met a client during the morning and on the way back to the hotel, went through a short thunderstorm. Hailstones the size of marbles rattled down on the taxi roof and drowned the noise of the engine.

At 2pm, just as I was about to set off again, the sky went black and there was a violent wind followed by lightening the like of which I had never seen before. Then followed torrential rain with some three inches falling in the space of one and a half hours. Electricity failed and everything came to a standstill. Part of the town was flooded to a depth of three feet and thousands of tiny frogs appeared from nowhere. For the date packers a storm like this could prove disastrous, as this was the time of year when the blossom was on the date palms.

Khorramshahr, the main date growing area, was seven miles away. It was a pleasant little town, and had a very English feel about it. This was possibly due to the fact that the oil refineries, at nearby Abadan were at one time owned by BP, and many English technicians came to live here, and influenced the way it was built. Streets were tree lined with pavements similar to an English market town. Sadly during the Iraq/Iran war the town was virtually destroyed.

The Karoun river, which runs into the Shatt Al Arab delta, divides the town in two, and on the right-hand bank the date plantations stretched as far as the eye could see. Within this area hundreds of farmers tended their own palms, and had contracts with the packers at harvest time.

At one of the packers, I was asked where I lived and when I said Bristol, the owner said he had a son at the Colston's School. When I said we lived right next to it, he asked me if I would take a letter to the Headmaster. I agreed and he wrote a short note and put it in an envelope.

Things were changing in the Iranian economy. A high import duty had been introduced to protect local manufacturers. Paul's customer Pars had installed their own printing machine. The only business we were likely to get now was from those clients who exported their goods and the date packers were exempt.

Getting about from one packer to another proved to be quite difficult as not all could provide transport to take me. So I had to rely on local taxis which seemed few and far between. Whilst standing on the roadside I noticed that there were frequent minibuses. I was joined by a local who waved one of these buses down, and indicated to me to get on. It appeared to be going in the direction I wanted, so I did. I showed the driver the name of the hotel I was staying in. He nodded and off we went. Soon we stopped and picked up a woman dressed in the black burka with her eyes just visible. She also had two smelly goats with her so it all got a little crowded. Apparently taxis are considered a luxury and were not as popular or as affordable by the locals as the minibuses.

It was time to go home. A KLM flight got me to Amsterdam where I connected to Heathrow.

I went round to Colston's School and delivered the letter to the headmaster. He opened it, read it and burst out laughing. My customer was asking that his son be given a beating to make him learn more!

Chapter 8

Nature and nature's laws lay hid in night
God said "Let Newton be" and all was light

Epitaph for Sir Isaac Newton

Getting back to the office was hard. I had reports to write, enquiries to action, orders to enter and early visits to London to see Mr Toby and other contacts. The number of orders that I had brought back proved that there was good business to be done and at last I was told by the Sales Director that I could be classified as an export representative. I felt that finally, finally, I had "arrived".

This promotion carried a salary increase and I knew that I would be able to provide better support for the family. Not that my salary was too impressive. Credit cards were now making an impact but Barclaycard and Mastercard were not accepted in the Middle East then, because of a presumed link with Israel. The only card accepted was American Express, although why this card was OK puzzled me. For future trips, I needed some back-up in case I found myself short of funds due to the very high cost of hotels. The problem then was that American Express would not issue a card to anyone with a salary of less than £15,000 which, I was a long, long way short of. The company gave me a covering letter explaining the situation and this did the trick and I got a card.

In 1976, Britain's economy was still in dire trouble.

Harold Wilson resigned suddenly as Prime Minister and was replaced by James Callaghan. The IRA was now mounting a bombing campaign on mainland UK. Britain and Iceland were engaged in a "cod" war and destroyers had been stationed in the North Sea to protect British trawlers. Political strife in Westminster in 1975 saw Margaret Thatcher oust Edward Heath as Leader of the Conservative opposition. The only bright note was that the first oil was extracted from the North Sea, and the Queen switched on the first pipeline bringing oil ashore.

The Middle East was rarely out of the news. Then, as today, it generally got a bad press. There was tension between Israel and Egypt and a resolution to the Palestinian question was as far off as it is today. In Saudi Arabia the King was assassinated. Civil war was breaking out in the Lebanon. On a PIA flight from Baghdad to Istanbul we landed briefly at Beirut. As we landed we could see smoke hanging over the surrounding areas. Over the Tannoy the Captain said that it was too dangerous to taxi to the airport terminal and that he intended to take off again. If anyone wanted to disembark he would arrange for them to do so but no luggage would be unloaded. Only one person decided to leave and a mobile staircase was brought out to get the man off. Then we were off without further delay.

Just a normal year in the region then! The world was such a troubled place that nowhere could be considered safe so I didn't see any reason why I shouldn't try to build on what I had already started.

Pakex is an international packaging exhibition, which takes place in Dusseldorf every four years. Although our company did not have a stand there, our parent company British Cellophane did. I persuaded them to let me base myself there for two days during the May show. I had to stay anonymous because a lot of their business was with other printers, but this was not a problem as I intended to go round the huge exhibition making contact with packaging machine manufacturers from other European countries. This worked a treat and I came away with many contacts that were to prove invaluable over the following years.

We would co-operate with them by supplying sample reels for testing before they sent their equipment to the Middle East. This proved popular with them, as well as their clients, and gave us a big advantage in securing orders.

From Dusseldorf I went to Frankfurt. One of my major clients in Iraq had come to nearby Wiesbaden to a Health Spa and had summoned all his suppliers to meet him there. We all were given an allotted time to meet him, but it was a very strange environment in which to do business.

In planning my flights I noticed that Pan American were operating a Boeing 747 from Frankfurt to Heathrow. At that time the largest aircraft that I had seen was a 707. I had seen the introduction of the "Jumbo" 747 on TV, and the size of it had caused quite a stir.

Pan Am Flight 001 was in itself part of aviation history. A "round the world flight" was a major innovation and quickly captured the American public's imagination. The first flight on a Lockheed Constellation aeroplane took place in 1947 from San Francisco flying west, touching down in Honolulu, Hong Kong, Bangkok, Delhi, Beirut, Istanbul, Frankfurt, London, and finally New York. Flight 002 started in New York, and travelled in the opposite direction landing at the same places but finishing in San Francisco.

What appealed to passengers was the fact that they could alight at any of the destinations, have a short stay, and then catch another 001 flight as it came through. The whole trip however had to be completed in 180 days so there was plenty of time for rich Americans to enjoy the pleasures of the Far East and Europe. Fight 001 in 1947, took 48 hours to circumnavigate the globe, but the arrival of the jet age changed that time scale.

I certainly had a shock when I saw the aircraft up close for the first time. It seemed to defy Newton's law of gravity that something so big could stay up in the air. The flight was fully booked with many American service personnel going back to the States. As the aircraft lumbered down the runway it seemed it would never get off the ground, but a smooth take off was achieved and my qualms disappeared. Even bigger aircraft are in the skies now. I saw the new A380 Airbus when it came on a demonstration flight over Bristol and it made the 747 look quite ordinary.

Chapter 9

Remember that time is money

BENJAMIN FRANKLIN – ADVICE TO A YOUNG TRADESMAN

As the summer of 1975 passed into autumn, I started to make my plans for further visits and sent off applications for various visas. It was also necessary, with the company's backing, to apply for a second passport. The London embassies of Middle East countries were notoriously slow in issuing visas, which meant that if a sudden trip to Europe were required, I would be in some difficulty as my passport would be in London.

Wanting to consolidate what had been achieved particularly in Yemen and Iraq, plus having a look at possibilities in the Gulf Emirates, required some tricky time management. I tried various combinations of flights and eventually came up with a fifteen day trip starting in Jeddah, then onward to Taiz, Abu Dhabi, Dubai, Kuwait, Iraq, and finally Turkey.

Turkey was an extra destination at the request of British Cellophane. They had supplied Cellophane to several dry battery manufacturers for wrapping small packs of batteries. Unfortunately during the transit of these batteries all over Turkey, movement had caused the contact points on the batteries to rub against the film and the moisture protection coating on the film had been rubbed off allowing moisture to corrode the batteries. British Cellophane was facing a big claim, but the problem needed a solution as well. Our company had equipment, which could coat Cellophane with polythene, and it was thought that this would be the answer. Trial material was sent out well in advance of my visit and I was to find out what the results had been.

Starting on November 1st, I travelled with British Airways, which had introduced a direct flight to Jeddah. Immigration procedures had changed and this time my passport was not taken away. No green channel again and Customs were very thorough. All English language newspapers were confiscated. Several Americans had been on the flight. They had brought videos with them, presumably to watch in their company's compounds. These too were confiscated despite loud protests.

It was for them an early introduction as to how restrictive life was going to be for them in Saudi Arabia. Foreigners employed by Saudi companies live in designated compounds. Whilst Christians are allowed to work, they are not allowed to worship. Churches are prohibited. No alcohol is permitted although it was often reported that illegal brewing took place in some of the compounds. Anyone involved in this would have had to keep a sharp look out for the religious police. They have great powers. Women are not allowed to drive, and foreign women must dress with arms and legs fully covered.

There was one story doing the rounds about the British Embassy. Diplomatic consignments bypassed Customs inspection and prohibited goods were allegedly brought in with a different description on the manifest. One day, the story goes, the Embassy got a telephone call from their clearing agent to say that a crate containing a "piano" had been dropped and that it was leaking! It was a good story anyway.

With no agent, I had to find my own way around. The man on the hotel reception desk was most helpful, and wrote down in Arabic, the names of the places I wanted to visit. I then stood outside on the pavement with my arm in the air and, as if by magic, three cars raced towards me. I knew that I would have to negotiate the fare. Three drivers looked at the first of my destinations and each demanded 20 Rials which was about £3. After some hard bargaining, I got one to accept 7 Rials, which is what the receptionist told me was the normal charge.

Some useful contacts were made during the day, and in the evening I had an appointment at the biscuit factory I had visited on my first trip. The place was still in a state of chaos and a lot of construction work was still going on, not only at the factory, but also on adjoining sites. Our first orders had arrived and were performing satisfactorily but so had the Italian material, which was also running well. The English manager was still there, but no mention was made of his proposal made on my first visit. It was clear that our prices were far higher than the Italian supplier and I later discovered that they were getting a big tax refund from the Italian Government to assist their exports. During our meeting the lights went out and we were plunged into darkness. I was told that this frequently happened as mechanical diggers chopped through the underground power cables. Our meeting finished by torchlight.

Next morning I went to the British Embassy to see the Commercial Attache. I explained what our business was about and that we knew that Saudi Arabia was working on a five-year plan to become more self-sufficient. Frankly he wasn't much help, definitely a "stiff upper lip" type who only seemed interested in major government projects. It was an attitude I was to find quite common in various British embassies around the region.

Two days in Jeddah was enough although I knew at

some stage I would need to go to Riyadh and Dammam on the east coast. With Saudi Arabia being the size of Europe, it was inevitable that industrial expansion would take place in these areas too, but Taiz was my next stop.

I don't think I should have been surprised that once again I encountered a problem with Yemen Airways. British Airways in London were at that time acting as booking agents for Yemenair and had issued my ticket. However when I presented the ticket at the check-in desk it was refused. I rushed round to the local BA office but they refused to issue another ticket saying that the original one was still valid. So it was back to Yemenair where I kicked up a tremendous fuss and eventually got them to accept it. Then to add insult to injury, they put the flight back four hours.

That meant we didn't get to Taiz until late afternoon, which left me with only one working day in the area. The road from the airport was now fully paved, and I learnt that the whole road from Taiz to Sanaa had now been completed since my first visit.

This time I had been booked in the grandly named Plaza Hotel next to the company office. I wasn't too impressed with my room. When I looked at the bed covers I could see bloodstains. Naturally I asked for them to be changed, and was told that the previous occupant had been bitten by a rat! When I went to the dining room that evening for a meal, the menu offered "Meat catlets" "Vegetable chicks" and for dessert, "Beach melba". I ordered a steak and it was surprisingly good.

I went to the factory early next day. As we exited through the old city gate we passed a column of women carrying large bundles of brushwood to sell in the market. I was told that they set out from the villages on top of the mountain, well before first light. A paved road had been constructed up the mountain but the women still preferred to use the old paths.

There were no problems in the factory this time and I noticed the machine, which had caused me all the problems before, now lying idle in a corner. It appeared that they had also run into problems with misshapen sweets, which caused the machine to jam, so they had switched all production to the twist machines.

Next morning I checked the flight time which should have been 11.15am but was told it was now 1.15pm. The company man, who was going to take me to the airport, offered to take me round the old town to fill in the time. In a letter to my wife, I wrote:

I had a good time with my camera and quite a few market stall holders posed. It was a real conglomeration of people, camels, goats, donkeys and produce. The market worked on the same principal as in Baghdad, that is with each trade having its own street. The fruit and fish section didn't half pong and I have never seen so many flies. You would have enjoyed the silk and cloth stalls, which were very colourful. Then there were the metal workers making knives and daggers like the one, which I brought home. Last of all were the cobblers, some of whom were making shoes out of old tyres.

I did notice a long queue of men at one stall and was told that they were waiting for a delivery of qat. This is a small leaf, which is mildly narcotic, and to which the majority of Yemeni men are addicted and are willing to pay a lot for.

I was to see many men with a noticeable lump of the stuff in their cheek, looking very glazed.

At Taiz airport chaos reigned. I was the only foreign passenger and the check-in staff asked me to wait whilst they sorted the Yemenis out. This was no simple task. As I had observed during my time in the Yemen, the men all wore the curved dagger as part of their dress and now they were being told to disarm and hand in the weapons. Most, if not all, were refusing to do this amidst loud protests and it took a soldier with a gun to calm things down. Reluctantly they handed in the daggers, all of which were tagged with the owner's name and the men were then taken outside and lined up.

Then the women, dressed from head to foot in the black burka, were taken one by one into a small room to be searched not without some very vocal protests. They too were lined up outside away from the men and then led to the aircraft. It was pretty obvious that the majority had never flown before and the cabin crew had quite a job getting them seated before allowing the men on. More problems occurred because some of the men had more than one wife, so there were furious arguments as to who was going to sit with whom. All these goings on I watched from one of the cabin crew's jump seats which they thought it best I occupy.

Finally, with everyone seated at last, we were ready for take off. As soon as the plane accelerated down the runway. Passengers on one side got up and crowded on the other side to wave to relatives. Nearly all the men were smoking and the cabin crew were going crazy trying to restore order. Even after take off they had to prevent one man from lighting a small paraffin stove in the aisle. Otherwise it was an incident free flight!

After landing at Sanaa, I was allowed off the plane first

and then watched as a real scrum developed in the baggage claim area as the men claimed their daggers. Everyone wanted to be first. My new suitcase was surviving well, if somewhat scratched already.

I had a three-hour wait to get the connecting flight to Abu Dhabi. My fellow passengers were Yemenis going to work in the Gulf area. All seemed to be taking all their worldly goods with them including huge radios. Their problem was that the weight of these possessions was way over the baggage allowance. So they were going outside the terminal trying to sell things to passers by. By the time we boarded, the departure hall was littered with discarded belongings especially blankets and foam mattresses.

Watching this made the time go quickly though. I also saw a woman dressed in the traditional burka, struggling with a yelling baby about one year old I guess. I watched as she went to the small airport shop and came back with, what I found out was a bottle of gripe water. She couldn't get the top unscrewed, so I indicated to her to let me try. I then handed it back and she poured the whole lot into a cup and gave it to the child. It drank the lot and went to sleep very quickly, with a contented look on its face.

Abu Dhabi seemed a very clinical sort of place. Everything was brand new and there was no character in the architecture. This was one of the seven emirates, which formed the United Arab Emirates in 1971. The area was still developing and beginning to realise the potential of its oil wealth of which Abu Dhabi was the greatest beneficiary, and in reality held the purse strings.

Moving on to Dubai next day, I found a very different atmosphere. The combination of old and new buildings clustered around the inlet waterway known as The Creek was very special. Hotels and offices bordered the wharves and on the quayside were stacked goods of all descriptions. Lorries, motor bikes, pick up trucks, freezers, tractors, furniture, cattle, goats, bales of cloth all brought in from Iran, Pakistan or India by small and large dhows. In amongst the waterway traffic, small ferries plied to and fro taking passengers across to the other side. It was a fascinating place to walk around.

My business at that time was with several bakeries and I also took a taxi to Sharjah, a separate state but only twenty minutes away further down the coast. Dubai was rapidly developing its reputation as being the leading emirate. Its duty free shop at the airport attracted many airlines to make a stop there on the way to or from Australia and the Far East.

There was jealousy among the emirate partners. Because Dubai had a large international airport, Sharjah decided that it too needed one even though there are only a few miles between the two states. Whereas Dubai was attracting flights from at least forty airlines, Sharjah was getting only two or three flights a day. Like Abu Dhabi it didn't have much character and the small town was centred around the port and oil terminals.

Next day I was off to Kuwait and beginning to feel like one of those American or Japanese tourists who "do" Britain in three days. I was glad too that I now had the American Express card. Two nights in Dubai had cost £180 and I made sure I kept the receipt for my expense claim!

Kuwait was proving to be a worthwhile market and on this visit I met Slaiman's American wife Donna and their two young daughters. It was a quick visit and next stop was Baghdad. We were now getting good repeat business, and new contacts were being made.

Four days in Iraq wasn't nearly enough to do all I would

have liked but I had to stick to my schedule, and there was much to take back to Bristol to action.

Baghdad to Istanbul, two of the most iconic cities, the latter where east meets west. Arriving in damp cold November meant that perhaps I didn't see it at its best, but it struck me immediately on the drive from the airport as a city full of energy, emphasised by the number of ferries, ships and naval shipping on the Sea of Marmara. I was staying at the Hilton, which was high up overlooking the Bosphorus, the narrow strait between the Black Sea and the Sea of Marmara, which connects Europe with Asia.

I had no appointments in the afternoon so, as it was at least dry, I went for a walk down the hill to have a look at the shipping. Just around the corner from the hotel, I passed a group of people on the pavement watching a man with a brown bear. He had it on a chain and was making it dance. This horrible practice was common and despite protests from animal welfare bodies, it was not banned until 1998.

As I reached the wall overlooking the narrow strait, a convoy of Russian warships was negotiating its way through the various ferries and small boats. In the November gloom, the ships' dark grey outlines looked very menacing, a reminder perhaps that the "Cold War" was very much a reality then.

Trials using our new material had gone well. Some contracts had already been agreed by telex so that our customers could apply for their import licences, so I thought my visit would be just to dot a few I's and cross a few T's. One customer however requested a further meeting on the morning of the day I was due to return to the UK. My flight was due at 1pm. The buyer, whom I normally dealt with, was Haluk Ide, a very nice chap who didn't give me a hard time in negotiations. He told me that the owner of the company wanted to meet me and I assumed, wrongly, that this was to be just a courtesy call.

I went to the office at 10am thinking that I still had plenty of time to make it to the airport for the check-in time. I sat at the head of a rectangular table with Mr Ide and the factory manager on each side. We were then joined by Mr Tatlici who sat opposite me at the other end of the table. Instead of the usual pleasantries, Mr Tatlici launched into a full scale rant about our prices. To say I was rather taken aback would be a bit of an understatement. Once I had recovered from the initial onslaught, I started to try and bring the discussion to a calmer point and find out what he was thinking. I then realised that he was comparing our prices with the plain Cellophane that his company had used before and which had caused them problems.

Time was ticking on and I had one eye on the clock, but he was still saying that he was paying too much. I knew exactly what our margins were and any reduction would not have been popular back home. I tried to get the quantity increased for a small percentage reduction, which would have left our margin the same. He wasn't satisfied and I wouldn't budge. Mr Tatlici was quite an intimidating fellow. Short in stature with jet black hair and a face well tanned and heavily creased. By now it was 11.30am and he showed no signs of stopping. I had run out of steam and with the airport over half an hour away, I knew I would miss my flight.

Then, quite suddenly and without warning, Mr Tatlici jumped up from his chair and came round the table towards me. I genuinely felt he was going to hit me but instead he grasped my hand, shook it vigorously, and said how much he had enjoyed the meeting. He then instructed Mr Ide to drive me to the airport. That was not the end of the surprises because on the way, Mr Ide stopped briefly at a shop owned by Mr Tatlici and I was given leather coats for my wife, son, and daughter.

I still didn't think I would catch my flight, but evidently Mr Tatlici had influence there too and a very late check-in proved no problem at all. I learnt sometime later that Mr Tatlici was one of Istanbul's most prominent businessmen with many company interests. He also had something of a reputation and one story concerned the wedding of one of his children. The reception was held at the Hilton and following a family tradition, guns were fired into the air. The only problem was that this was done in the ballroom causing £10,000 worth of damage!

Mr Sarkis in Baghdad had asked me to deliver a letter to a relative who had a shop in the famous covered market. An amazing place it is too and even for someone who doesn't like shopping, I found it fascinating. Each tier of the market has its own number and had to be cross-referenced against the shop number. I seemed to be continually climbing up the alleyways between the tiers until I eventually found the relevant tier. I walked along and found the shop, which sold beautiful onyx ornaments. I delivered the letter and Mr Sarkis' relative was most grateful. He insisted I stay for tea and then presented me with several onyx ornaments.

So this trip came to an end and had proved that there was much still to do. There were lots more places to visit and 1976 was the time to do it.

Chapter 10

Men will wrangle for religion...
CHARLES COLTON 1780–1832

"BULLSHIT". The letters of the word were at least two centimetres high. They leapt from the inside flyleaf of a Bible that I had found on the bedside table in my room at the Sheraton Hotel in Kuwait.

I don't really know why I had picked the Bible up in the first place. I had arrived fairly late in the evening from Baghdad, having ground through a long immigration queue and then a very thorough customs check.

All I really wanted to do was have a shower and get to bed as I had a busy day coming up. I suppose curiosity got the better of me, as I had not expected to find a Bible in this Middle Eastern country. Obviously the discovery of this Bible had been too much for a previous occupant of the room, but I wondered what had prompted the outburst. Was it a Muslim who had objected? There was a copy of the Quran in the room as well, so I discounted that theory. Perhaps it was an atheist who objected, but the Quran had not been vandalised.

Whatever the reason, my tiredness had disappeared and had been replaced by my mind searching for answers of which there were none that made any sense. Even now, more than thirty five years on, this incident is fresh in my mind and I often wonder what happened to the person who wrote that offensive word. I'll never know.

As I have already mentioned, I was surprised to find a Bible in the room especially after my visits to Saudi Arabia left me with the impression that it was banned in all Middle Eastern countries. Not so it would appear.

Closer examination showed that the Bible had been placed in the room courtesy of the Gideon's Society. This was new to me. I later found out that Gideon Bibles can be found in many hotels around the world.

The idea came from two American businessmen who met in Boscobel, Wisconsin in 1899. The two men, John H Nicholson and Samuel E Hill were forced to share a room when Boscobel was hosting a large convention, and hotel accommodation was at a premium. They had never met before and, having got talking, found that each had a deep Christian faith. They thought it would be a good idea to places Bibles in hotel rooms in America and agreed to follow up the idea after they parted. It took a while but more like minded contacts were made and Gideons International was formed.

The first Bibles were placed in the Superior Hotel, Superior, Montana in 1908. Since then, the organisation has distributed Bibles in over 94 languages to 194 countries in the world. Why the name Gideon? Gideon was a man willing to do whatever God asked of him. Humility and a deep faith were his characteristics, and Gideon members strive to emulate this.

On my first visit to Saudi Arabia, I had obtained a copy of a pamphlet from the Board of Trade [now The Dept of Trade and Industry] giving hints for businessmen about to go to Saudi Arabia. Amongst the usual advice about health, clothing, money, and climate was a statement that Bibles are not permitted neither were any Christian symbols such as crosses or wooden carvings.

I wouldn't have taken a Bible anyway and don't wear a cross. Landing cards required a declaration of religion and

I entered Christian. Although I regard myself as a practising Christian, I recognise my own failings. I don't read the Bible, but hear readings on Sundays. My view on Christianity is at best simplistic. The two great commandments are to "Love God and your neighbour as yourself". The 8am Holy Communion service on Sundays helps me to focus on the week ahead, but I have little time for the pomp and ceremony that goes on in the high church.

In the Yorkshire village where I grew up as a boy in the 1940s, I went to the local church like most folk did. This ensured I could get into the local youth club. For me the highlight of the church year was the annual visit of a missionary. These men spent three years abroad, often in difficult circumstances, and were allowed home then for three months leave. However they were required to visit churches up and down the land to tell of their work, and presumably drum up funds for further periods abroad.

Religious education in my school was totally boring. In morning assembly we lustily sang hymns like *Onward! Christian Soldiers* (marching as to war). It seemed that anyone who wasn't a Christian was a heathen and destined for hell. I didn't know any better then.

Missionaries were far more interesting. It wasn't so much about their Christian message, but the picture they painted about the far off places to which they had been sent. They brought various artefacts with them and grainy photographs or, better still, slides which they projected in the church hall.

One man, Wilfred Cartlidge, brought a stuffed cobra, which terrified the small children. Kenneth Platt who had served in Panama brought a shark's backbone. Rev. Mellor wrote in my autograph book "To a brave man even a blade of grass is a weapon". These men were heroes in our young eyes. I didn't pay much attention to the fact that they were trying to convert people in far off lands to Christianity.

So my foray into the big wide world not only had to be a steep learning curve, but also I had to understand the sensitivity of each country's culture and customs, and most importantly its religion.

On the face of it, although this may offend many, and I apologise if it does, I can see little difference in the basic concepts of Christianity and Islam. Christians follow the teachings of Jesus and the link to God whilst Muslims follow the teaching of Muhammad again with the link to God. With God at the centre of both faiths, and a command to follow a life of goodness, where did it all go wrong?

By the time Muhammad was born around AD570–71, Christianity had spread northwards and westwards from Jerusalem. The land now called Saudi Arabia, was sparsely populated by a few wandering tribes. The western side had one of the main caravan routes along which merchants brought camel trains bearing goods bound for the north. Mecca was a wealthy merchant town and a regular stopping place for the traders bringing gold, gems, silks, and spices such as frankincense and myrrh from Yemen, India, Persia, and Africa.

The Jews, with their reputation as traders, had established themselves along the trading routes. Their Old Testament religion contrasted to the multi-idol based religions of the local tribes. Those who had embraced the new Christian faith were also part of the local scene.

As well as being a trading centre, Mecca was also a religious centre in that it held the Kaaba black stone. It was guarded by the Quraysh tribe, to which Muhammad's family belonged. The history of the Kaaba goes back into the mists of time. The stone was said to have been placed there by Abraham and was a gift from Heaven. It became the site of pilgrimage for all the tribes regardless of which particular God they followed such as the moon, the sun or the stars.

Muhammad's early life had been marred by tragedy as his father died before he was born. His mother Aminah died when he was only six years old. His uncle, Abu Talib then took over the responsibility of raising him. Abu Talib was a trader and took the young Muhammad with him on the caravan convoys. It was on one of these journeys that Muhammad met a Nestorian monk who saw something very special in Muhammad, and predicted that he would become a great prophet.

Into adulthood, and Muhammad became a trader in his own right. He was an influential member of the Traders Guild in Mecca. On his journeys he met Jews and Christians, and would discuss religion with them.

Later he was employed by Khadijah, a wealthy widow, to look after her caravan trade. Although she was fifteen years older than Muhammad, they married when he was twenty five.

When he was about forty, and by now, a figure of great importance in the Mecca community, he became very unhappy about the irreligious behaviour of the local people. He would spend time in contemplation on Mount Hirah, which is three miles from Mecca. It was during one of these times of quiet meditation that he claimed he heard the voice of Allah who gave him messages to pass on to others.

Whilst his family supported his new teaching, his reception by the people of Mecca was anything but positive. He was accused of being a fortune teller, and some considered that he had gone mad.

As hostility increased towards him and the few converts he had managed to make, Muhammad realised that he would have to leave Mecca if he was to fulfil his destiny. He travelled to Medina where his teachings were well received with the emphasis on the idea of one God/Allah and the rejection of idolatry.

So it was here in AD622 that Islam was established, and in the next ten years before his death in AD632, the teaching and rules of Islam were written down in the Quran for the followers to learn by heart. Muslims [those who submit to God's will] were now told to face Mecca when praying, and not Jerusalem as before.

Muhammad's teachings did not find favour with the Jews or Christians, and initially at least, he accepted their right to follow the teaching of Judaism or Jesus. Conflict between the Jews and Muslims soon occurred because the Jews refused to recognise Muhammad as a true prophet.

This challenge to the truth of Islam was to be at the centre of countless wars and history tells of many conflicts through the centuries. Christianity had already taken a firm foothold throughout Europe, and Islam spread throughout Arabia and North Africa.

I do not propose to add to the on-going debate about the two religions and I have only given the briefest of outlines to the beginnings of Islam because of the significance to the places I visited.

In the short time I had been travelling, I had learned to respect prayer times. There was a story about the M1 soon after it opened. A police car on patrol stopped when it found a car on the hard shoulder and two men on their knees praying. I had been in taxis in the Middle East when the driver has stopped to pray by the side of the road. In meetings I had seen my customer halt negotiations at prayer time, take a prayer mat out of his desk and perform his prayers in the office. I had no problem with that. I also made sure that I avoided the special holidays and religious festival times and in particular, the fasting month of Ramadan.

Christianity is not short of controversy. Just look at the

divide between Protestants and Catholics. Islam too has two main branches of the religion, Sunnis and Shias constantly at loggerheads.

But it is only in Saudi Arabia that there is a total ban on Christian practices. Indeed if a Muslim were to convert to Christianity and be caught, then he could face a sentence of death. Foreign nationals can register with their embassy, and it is common practice for informal services to take place behind closed doors.

Elsewhere in the Middle East, because of the large number of "guest workers" Christian worship is tolerated. There are strong Christian communities in Lebanon, Jordan, Syria, Iraq, and Egypt. I was aware that these fall into the Anglican Diocese of Jerusalem. On my travels I took with me a paperback book entitled *Journey for a Soul*, written by George Appleton who was, from 1968–1974, Archbishop of Jerusalem and the Middle East. This is a collection of sayings, prayers, and thoughts of many people of all faiths, offering an insight onto the problems of the world and its people. I found it a source of help and I still have it, although it is very travel stained.

So, what happened to the previous occupant of my room? Did he leave a trail of abuse in Bibles in all the hotels he stayed in? It seems that through the ages, and still today, when religion and culture clash, it becomes a complex matter. Throw in politics as well, and complex becomes explosive.

I started this chapter with part of a quotation by Charles Caleb Colton. The full quotation reads:

Men will wrangle for religion, write for it, fight for it, die for it. Anything but live for it!

How very true!

Chapter 11

History repeats itself
19TH CENTURY

1976 and the early part of 1977 were a time to consolidate what had already been achieved, particularly in Yemen and Iraq. I was only too aware that our competitors from Italy, Germany, France and also our rivals in the UK, were targeting the Middle East. Our customers needed to know that I would be turning up at regular intervals to help progress their business.

In Kuwait however the situation was far from clear. There was some unrest, and the Emir, fearing a Beirut type uprising, suspended the Parliament. When I arrived in March 1977 an uneasy calm existed. I was though delighted and very relieved to see that our agent Slaiman was now back in Kuwait. He had gone to Beirut early 1976 and as far as his office and myself were concerned, simply disappeared. After almost one year he managed to get out safely, but the experience had taken its toll. He had lost weight, and looked quite gaunt. He had been caught up in the fighting, taken refuge, and had no means of letting anyone know where he was.

Slaiman's wife Donna has sent me an account of their experience in Beirut at this time and has kindly allowed me to use the following extracts.

We went to live in Beirut in 1973 so that I could attend the American University of Beirut, School of Nursing. I had a Diploma in nursing and the plan was that Slaiman would settle me and our two daughters Rania age 1½ and Tayma age 7 months into a place in Beirut. Once established Slaiman would return to his job in Kuwait and I would remain in Beirut to complete the degree requirements. With hindsight now I can say that we were truly naïve to the politics of Lebanon and the powder keg that was about to explode.

Slaiman returned to Kuwait and would visit every weekend from Thursday to Saturday.

On April 13th 1975 a bus load of Palestinian workers were ambushed and killed by Phalangist militia. The daily skirmishes that ensued after this event eventually led to a civil war. The skirmishes were in pockets of the city and one learned what areas to avoid.

In 1976 during one of Slaiman's trips to Beirut, the airport was closed due to shelling. The situation deteriorated. Neighbourhoods were sectioned off between the east and the west. The green line and no man's land between them was a war zone. Slaiman grew a beard and purposely spoke Arabic with a Lebanese accent. He tried to blend in. I spoke Arabic with broken grammar so I sounded like a foreigner. I told them that I was Polish living in Beirut.

From early 1976 till summer 1977 we lived without electricity except for the few hours that would come once a week. We subsequently would draw water from a well beneath the building for washing, bathing etc.

During this time we had an Eid holiday and Slaiman went out to get some fresh vegetables at a local market. Sometime later I heard a knock at the door and he was there with blood all over him. He explained that a rocket attack had taken place and he was grazed by shrapnel on his leg and neck. However another poor bystander was not so fortunate. He was more severely wounded. He was bleeding from the right side of his neck and holding the area with his left hand. The man did not know if he was going to make it. He had asked some persons in a home nearby for assistance and they told him to go away. Slaiman cared for him and via civil defence transport, took him to hospital for treatment. The man, a member of the Druze militia, survived and a couple of days later Slaiman went to visit him in hospital. He was surprised to learn that Slaiman was a Kuwaiti. He told him "you mean to say that there are Kuwaitis like that" and was so grateful to Slaiman.

He was angry and told Slaiman that he was going to have his revenge and blow up the house that had refused him help. Slaiman asked him not to do this but later revisited the site of the rocket attack and the building was no longer there. Slaiman never saw the man again.

During this time I was called upon to help with some 100 patients at the hospital who were hit by rockets. I still remember the blood and the shrapnel wounds. With only two ventilators, so *many were put in a section to die and it was in that section that I went to comfort the young patients. I got into an argument with someone who was removing a watch from a dying person. I can still feel the outrage I felt. It is an indelible mark on my psyche what misery people can inflict on others.*

The University remained opened. Tests and exams were not postponed due to any fighting. In August 1977 I completed the requirements of the degree course. The situation in Beirut was now considerably calmer relative to the previous rough year. With the airport reopening Slaiman felt comfortable enough to return to Kuwait and we were optimistic that peace would follow.

It is certainly a remarkable story of a family caught up in a terrible situation. During this period of almost twelve months Slaiman, Donna and their two small daughters had survived against all odds. As Donna says, "We were a family together going through rough times". Donna also got a Masters Degree in Public Health and the family was finally reunited in Kuwait in September 1978.

We also added to our family in 1977 with the welcome arrival of another son. We now had three sons and a daughter, which made a great family.

When preparing for a trip towards the end of 1977, Paul asked me to add on a couple of days to go to Teheran. Now that a 100% import duty had been applied to many items, it was possible that a deal could be done with a local printer to import material that could not be made in Iran and would therefore be exempt.

Teheran was a bewildering city. It is much bigger than Baghdad, and if I thought that traffic chaos was bad there, then it was ten times worse here. Pollution levels were extreme and it hung over the city like a grey shroud.

There was something very familiar too about many of the cars on the streets. They looked very like the British Hillman Hunter cars, which were a popular model in the UK in the 1970s. I found that they were one and the same. In 1967 the Coventry based Rootes Company began exporting the model in kit form, and it was assembled in Iran by Khodro Industrial Group and renamed the Paykan.

Iran, in 1977, was still a monarchy. The Shah of Persia, Mohammad Reza Pahlavi, was head of a secular run state, and the monarchy had been in existence since the founding of the Persian Empire by Cyrus the Great. The 2500th Anniversary was celebrated in lavish style in 1971. Such was the extravagance of the celebrations, said to have cost $100million,that demonstrations occurred, highlighting the impoverished state of a large percentage of the population. At that time, although Teheran was a modern, well equipped capital city, the bulk of Iran's population were living in the countryside in primitive conditions.

The Shah's pro-western foreign policy was already attracting much criticism particularly from the Shia clergy. He had a feared secret police, the Savak, to take care of dissidents. It was thought that over 2000 political prisoners were being held in prison.

So my arrival in Teheran at this time to check what was happening in the local economy was quite opportune. Our agent, Bijan Rafiee, was an extremely likeable man with a very optimistic outlook on life. After some meetings during the day, which more or less confirmed that we had no chance

111

of doing further business in this market, I went for a meal with Bijan and his charming wife in one of Teheran's top restaurants. Inside, I could not help noticing the contrast between very well dressed and obviously affluent men and women and the majority of the people we had passed on the way to the restaurant. The women in the restaurant dressed western style. No sign of the burka here.

When I asked Bijan about his optimistic view of things in view of the growing opposition to the Shah's regime, I got a surprising answer. He said that each year he and his wife went on a pilgrimage to Mashad. Mashad is situated in the north east of Iran, some 530 miles from Teheran, and is the country's second largest city. It is also one of the most holy cities for Shia Muslims. Here they would pray that good things would happen for them in the next twelve months, and Bijan claimed that everything that they had asked for had come to fruition.

The opportunity for me to go on from Teheran to Afghanistan came about as a result of my connections with a packaging machine company in Leeds. My contact tipped me off about a confectionery company in Kabul that was planning to build a new factory. The negotiations were being conducted through an office in Camden, North London. Quite a shock awaited me after I had made contact as the address turned out to be a shop not an office. The shop owner, a Mr Moradoff, sold very expensive fur and leather coats all made in Afghanistan. It was one of his relatives who was planning to build the confectionery factory, and he was negotiating on their behalf. I had no difficulty in finalising a deal to cover the packaging, and as I was going to Teheran, said I was willing to go to Kabul to meet his relatives and see how the factory was progressing.

Flight IR 820 left at the horribly early hour of 4.30am on Thursday morning. This meant being at Teheran airport at 2.30am so at least I didn't have to worry about traffic jams. Having located the check in desk area I found it crowded with Afghans all trying to check in at once. All seemed to be carrying large blankets, suitcases, miscellaneous paraphernalia, and smoking heavily. I appeared to be the only foreigner travelling.

Then I spotted another European, a short man, struggling with two huge suitcases. Making my way over to him, I asked if he wanted some help and found out that he was English, and what's more a Yorkshireman. I guess he was around sixty years old, and even at that unearthly hour of the morning, was smartly dressed in sharp contrast to my scruffy appearance. Richard Hanen was Managing Director of Hanen and Akeroyd Ltd from Bramley near Leeds. They made fine textiles. We got talking and found that we were both due to stay at the Intercontinental Hotel in Kabul.

As we were the only two foreigners on the flight, we managed to get seats together, but only after Mr Hanen had paid a hefty excess luggage charge on his two suitcases which contained all his samples of cloth.

I don't think I had quite appreciated how big a country Afghanistan is. The flight to Kabul in the far east of the country took three hours arriving at 7.30am.

It was instantly obvious that something was wrong as we landed. As the aircraft taxied towards the terminal building, we could see soldiers and armoured vehicles on the apron. The cabin crew made no attempt to open the doors and we were kept waiting for nearly one hour. Then we were allowed to leave the aircraft and proceeded to the terminal building watched closely by the soldiers. Fortunately there was a separate immigration desk for foreign nationals so Richard and I were through quickly, and customs only took a few moments as our luggage was already waiting in the baggage hall.

However that's as far as we got, for when we reached the Arrivals Hall, we found the exit locked and guarded by soldiers. We managed to find someone who spoke English and we were told that the Minister of Planning had been shot dead that morning and Kabul was in "lock down".

I suppose being the only two foreigners around, we rather stood out from the crowd. After quite a while, we were approached by a military man who looked like an officer. He asked where we were staying and we told him that we were booked in at the Intercontinental. He left us and a few minutes later he came back and beckoned to us to follow him. He led us outside to a taxi, which he had commandeered, and with a military jeep as escort we were driven to the Intercontinental on the edge of Kabul overlooking the city. Welcome to Afghanistan.

The history of Afghanistan has always been turbulent and still is. After fighting the British in three wars over a period of 103 years. Britain was desperate to keep the trade route open between what is now Pakistan and Afghanistan and much of the fighting was around the famous and strategic Khyber Pass, which was the only way through the mountains. Afghanistan finally achieved full independence in 1929. It remained a monarchy until 1973 when a revolution took place and a Republic was declared. A power struggle then ensued between various political factions, and at the time of our arrival, the country was being run by Presidential decree with the National Assembly suspended.

The Intercontinental Hotel was in a superb location

looking down towards Kabul over a forested area and beyond to the Baghe Bala, once the summer palace of the Royal family, but now converted to a restaurant. The city is situated some 5900ft above sea level, and is one of the highest capital cities in the world. As I looked out, I could see it was surrounded by snow capped mountains and the winter snows would soon be arriving at the lower levels. It was though, bitterly cold.

With nothing moving in Kabul, my plans to meet the potential customer that day were well and truly scuppered. Next day, Friday, was prayer day and the weekend, so that left me only Saturday to finalise everything as I was due to leave early on Sunday. There was nothing for it, but to write off the day and hope that some sort of normality would return after Friday prayers. I did get a phone call saying that all things being equal, I would be collected first thing on Saturday and taken to see the customer.

Friday began with the rain absolutely pouring down, and it continued all day. I had harboured thoughts of perhaps doing a bit of sightseeing, but these quickly disappeared what with the weather and the tense situation in the city.

Richard Hanen, on the other hand, had managed to make contact with his potential customers, and some had agreed to come to the hotel to see him and his products. He asked me to lend a hand, which I was pleased to do. It proved very entertaining. A succession of Afghan businessmen came during the day, and after each visit, Richard's room was strewn with cloth samples, which I collected and straightened out before the next client arrived. Using an interpreter I think Richard was able to create a good deal of interest in his products, and the day passed very quickly.

Saturday morning, and thankfully the rain had stopped. I got a call from the hotel reception to say that someone was waiting for me in the lobby. The man spoke no English and we went outside to a battered pick up truck with a driver already in it. Then, sandwiched between the two men, with my large briefcase on my knees, we drove for about twenty minutes to a hilly area on the outskirts of Kabul.

We stopped outside a small breeze block building, and inside I met the owner and his brother who did speak good English. I could already smell sugar being boiled as we went in to an adjoining area. Here a large copper vat was boiling away with the mixture, but what immediately caught my eye were the thousands of ants crawling up the side of the vat to get at the sticky overflow, with most perishing in the attempt.

The mixture eventually was poured onto cooling trays, then rolled out and formed into sweets, again with ants everywhere. The finished product was then put into polythene bags for transport to the market. The brothers recognised the primitive nature of their business and, as I had been informed in London, planned to fully mechanise. Next to their building, foundations had already been laid for a factory, and they planned to confirm their order with the supplier in Leeds in 1978. I had brought some design ideas for their sweet wrappers with me. One was selected and a deal done. Fortunately I was not offered any sweets, and after the customary tea, I was taken back to the hotel.

I now had the afternoon free. Richard was still busy so, as traffic seemed to be moving about normally, I decided to try and have a look around the local market to see if there were any other potential clients in the area. In other countries I had found this a useful way of getting information. I asked the hotel to organise a driver. They told me that a large part of Kabul was still closed off, but there was a driver prepared to take me.

I don't think the driver was prepared for me wandering

about among the market stalls when we reached the commercial centre of Kabul. Here was a mass of people, cars, pick–up trucks, vans, sheep, goats, chickens, cattle all vying for space with the various shops whose produce spread outwards over the pavements into the road. The noise was deafening. I realised that there was not much point in my looking for marketing opportunities here, as trading was being done in the most basic of fashions. People didn't seem to mind me taking photographs, but the driver was getting distinctly nervous and ushered me back into the car at every opportunity.

Moving further on we came across some more shops slightly more modern, but here I saw a butcher's shop with animal carcasses hanging over the front just a few feet away from an open sewer. Flies were everywhere. The appearance of a few soldiers was enough for my driver to decide this was not the place to be, so he said he would take me to any of the few local places of interest that were still open.

I suppose that given Afghanistan's history, a mausoleum was as good a place as any to start. This was the tomb of Amir Abdur Rahman, a dynamic ruler in the 19th century. The impressive white marbled, blue domed building is in a park on a hill overlooking Kabul.

Next stop was the Babur Gardens. Babur was the founder of the Moghul Dynasty in the 16th century. He had the gardens laid out for his pleasure and relaxation, and he so loved the place that he left instructions that he be buried there after his death which was in 1530. This wish was carried out by his Afghan wife Bibi Mobaraka, and a tomb commemorates him in the gardens.

By now it was getting dark and the driver was getting more and more agitated. We drove back to the Intercontinental passing several Government offices and roads still cordoned off and manned by the military.

I had a meal with Richard that evening. He was staying for a little longer. Early next morning I left for Kabul Airport to catch Ariana Flight FG70 leaving at 9am direct to Heathrow. My departure was in complete contrast to my arrival. No military presence and all seemed back to normal. So relaxed was the atmosphere that a security guard spotting my camera bag did not object to me taking a photograph of the aircraft. To say I was surprised is an understatement, as taking pictures in airports is normally forbidden.

The Flight left on time and once again I was the only foreigner on board. As we flew westwards I had a clear view from my window seat of the mountainous terrain below all the way to Iran. I looked forward to visiting Afghanistan again once the factory was open.

Alas, it was not to be. The political strife, part of which I had witnessed on my visit, escalated and early in 1978 there was another coup. This was backed by Russia, but such was the opposition to the new President, that Russia decided to prop up the regime and sent in 100,000 troops to occupy the country. Some estimates give the number of Afghans killed as up to two million whilst six million refugees fled to Iran and Pakistan.

The Russians became bogged down in a ten year war with local tribes and totally failed to quell them. Russian losses were horrific and in 1989, Russian President Michail Gorbachev ordered the withdrawal of all Russian forces. There then followed years of civil war with the Taliban eventually taking control in 1996 plunging the country back into the Middle Ages.

Needless to say, my contact with the client in Kabul

ceased, and I have no idea what happened to the two brothers.

After 9/11, the politicians of America, Britain and other countries decided that it was in their "national" interest to declare war on the Taliban whom they accused of harbouring Al Qaeda.

Since then in over ten years, attempts by NATO to bring stability to Afghanistan, by flooding the country with thousands of troops, have failed miserably. No figures are ever released of the number of Taliban killed or the number of Afghan civilians who have perished. The number of Afghans fleeing the country continues apace and the sad sight of seeing dead British soldiers being repatriated through Royal Wootton Basset and now Brize Norton, has been a regular feature on our television screens, with their families devastated as a result.

I recently watched a series on the BBC called *Our War*. It was filmed by British soldiers in action in Afghanistan. It reminded be of an account I had read about an earlier military engagement in that country. It read:

The fighting was fierce with the enemy contesting the advance, yard by yard through orchards and walled gardens in the village and then from house to house.

The Seaforth Highlanders and Gurkhas bore the brunt of the attack and the Seaforths lost their new Commander, Colonel Brownlow who had distinguished himself in the campaign. Colonel Roberts then pushed forward with a reserve brigade as there was fear of a counter attack.

The enemy made a most determined stand turning their guns on the British from entrenched positions. However a brilliant dash by Major White and some of the Gordon Highlanders drove the enemy in headlong flight from their positions and decided the issue.

In true Afghan fashion the enemy vanished into the surrounding area, reappearing as peaceful farmers.

Perhaps I should have mentioned earlier that the above account was written in 1879!!

Will we never learn? Don't politicians ever study history. What does the future hold for Afghanistan? I certainly don't know. I do know that flooding the country with foreign troops has never worked. Now all the talk is about withdrawing and leaving the mess to the Afghans to sort out. Whatever happens there is a lot more blood to be spilt, unfortunately.

Camel on the way to Sanaa

Fishmarket at Muscat Harbour, Oman

Fruit and veg, Muscat Souk, Oman

Taiz from Hotel

Taiz Town Gate

Knife and clock seller, Taiz Market, Yemen

Great Pyramid and Sphinx, Giza, Egypt

Inside the Siq, Petra

The Creek, Dubai

House on a rock, Yemen

Al Rashafiya Mosque, Taiz, Yemen

Treasury at Petra, Jordan

14th Ramadan Mosque,
Baghdad

Street traders, Kabul

The Lion of Babylon

Ishtar Gate, Babylon

The Towers, Kuwait

Al Bunnia Mosque, Baghdad

Chapter 12

It's an ill wind that blows nobody good

<small>PROVERB</small>

The late 1970s were to see the face of the Middle East once again change significantly. One face, which dominated the world's media, was that of the Ayatollah Khomeini. The situation in Iran had become increasingly volatile. The Shah's enemies, apart from various political elements, now included the all powerful Shia clergy. Widespread demonstrations and riots broke out, but all attempts to quell the unrest proved unsuccessful.

Recognising the overwhelming opposition to his rule, and perhaps remembering what had happened to the royal family in Iraq, the Shah abdicated early in 1979 and left the country with all his family.

On February 1st 1979, Ayatollah Khomeini returned from the exile, which had been imposed on him by the Shah, with the co-operation of Saddam Hussein. By February 11th, forces supporting the Ayatollah had seized power and he was declared Leader of the Islamic Republic of Iran.

These events sent shock waves around the Middle East, especially those countries, which were still ruled by monarchies such as Saudi Arabia, Jordan, Oman, Kuwait, and all the Emirates. Almost immediately, Ayatollah Khomeini launched a blistering attack of words on these countries and urged all

Shia Muslims to rise up and declare Islamic republics in their own country and follow full Sharia law.

Security was stepped up, particularly in Saudi Arabia, and several plots were uncovered. The Ayatollah's special venom however was directed at Saddam Hussein who had ejected him from Iraq as part of a treaty signed with the Shah. Sunni Muslims made up the majority of the ruling powers in Iraq, and Shia Muslims in the south of Iraq were being urged to rise up and fight. Within months, Iraq and Iran were at war, a war which was to last ten years with dreadful casualties on both sides, and which virtually bankrupted both countries.

The rest of the Middle East looked on nervously, dreading that they too might get drawn into the conflict.

Part of the hostile invective from the Ayatollah was directed personally at King Khalid who, as well as being the absolute ruler of the House of Saud, also had the title Custodian of the Two Holy Mosques. These are Masjid Al Haram in Mecca and Masjid Al Nabawi in Medina. The main criticism was the way in which pilgrims were treated on the Haj, the most important event in any Muslim's life.

I had seen something of the trials that pilgrims encountered on some of my visits. On yet another trip to Yemen, I was due to travel from Sanaa to Jeddah. There was what seemed to be the customary flight delay, which should have been around lunchtime. The reason was linked to the number of pilgrims wanting to travel to Jeddah for the Haj. A separate charter flight had been laid on. I was transferred to this flight and realised that all my fellow passengers were men, all shaven headed and wearing the traditional pilgrim's garb of white towelling robes. This time the traditional daggers had been left behind. Weapons are not allowed to be carried in Mecca.

Departure time became unclear and I could see from the

departure lounge that something was going on outside. Sanaa Airport was situated out in the countryside away from the city. I went up to a viewing area on the roof and could see a lot of military activity setting up roadblocks on the route to the airport.

There was no one to ask what was going on but as I watched, I noticed on the horizon, a great cloud of dust from which started to emerge a convoy of trucks, cars, and pick up vans all heading on the road towards Sanaa.

There was tension in the air as the convoy neared the vicinity of the airport. The trucks were full of tribesmen all shouting and waving. I did wonder if yet another revolution was happening. After all, since I first started coming to Yemen four years ago, the photograph of the President, compulsory on all office and factory walls, had changed a few times!

Fortunately for us anyway, the convoy showed no signs of slowing down and headed towards Sanaa. What was going on I have no idea, but there must have been at least 500 vehicles on the road.

Our charter flight finally left in the late afternoon with me again occupying a cabin crew seat. Once airborne, the passengers started a repetitive prayer chant, which they kept going all the way on the one hour flight to Jeddah.

On landing, I was allowed to leave the aircraft first, so was through immigration quickly. I then made my way to the baggage retrieval area. I waited, and waited, and waited, but there was no sign of any baggage coming along the carousel. I also realised that none of my fellow passengers were there either.

Somewhat concerned, I made my way to the Yemen Airways desk only to find it closed. The adjoining Saudi Airways desk was manned and I asked if they could help me sort out my predicament. They were very helpful and phoned a Yemen Airways representative who must have been home by now. After a while he came back to the airport and agreed to help me find my suitcase. He said that what had probably happened was that my suitcase had been taken off with all the Yemenis' luggage and taken to the Haj holding area in the airport complex. All we had to do now was to find out where this area was.

It was now very dark outside as we walked beyond the terminal. It was impossible to tell exactly where we were, but it was somewhere near the airport perimeter. My guide had a torch and as we walked, we passed groups of people huddled together in the cold night air. It appeared that each group had come from a different country that day, and were waiting for clearance before going to Mecca next day. They all looked pretty miserable and very uncomfortable.

We passed group after group and just as I was beginning to think we would be unsuccessful, we found the Yemenis. They must have been perished dressed only in their white robes. A rummage by torchlight through the pile of baggage soon located my suitcase much to my relief. We made our way back to the terminal building, and another rigorous Customs search seemed a reasonable price to pay.

When you consider that in the main period of the Haj Pilgrimage, several million Muslims descend on Mecca, mostly via Jeddah. They come by air, sea and land from all over the world. All men are required to dress in the simple white robes. The principle is that the simplicity of the robes makes all men equal regardless of wealth or position. Women are expected to wear their normal burka. This mass arrival gives the Saudi Arabian authorities a huge logistical problem. Massive fleets of buses transport pilgrims to Mecca. Hotels are always full, and I would imagine that most sleep out on the streets. I also witnessed some very sick people crawling on their hands and knees towards the bus terminal.

I have grown to admire the sheer determination of these pilgrims to fulfil their life's ambition of getting to Mecca at least once in their lifetime. For many it must have taken a big financial sacrifice. I remember seeing Turkish pilgrims camped around fires at the side of the road in Baghdad. Their 2000 mile journey was in clapped out old buses and must have taken several days.

The criticism levelled at the Saudi authorities made them decide to build a special Haj terminal at Jeddah and there is now a magnificent building in place.

Back to 1979 though, and not long after I had left Jeddah, Iranian pilgrims encouraged by Ayatollah Khomeini, occupied the Grand Mosque and declaring Islamic fundamentalism, refused to leave. The siege was ended when Saudi troops stormed the building leaving many dead, and captured a lot of prisoners. A total of 178 were executed.

This incident shocked the world of Islam, and difficulties over the handling of such vast numbers of people have been a continuing problem, giving rise to much criticism despite the Saudi authorities best efforts. Stampedes have killed many and the suspicion that Iran was causing many of the problems led to number restrictions. There was also an outbreak of meningitis, which forced the Saudi authorities to insist on the production of a vaccination certificate when applying for a visa. Yet another jab for me!

In 1985 Saudi troops had to break up a riot in Mecca which left 300 Iranians and 200 other nationalities dead. King Fahad had succeeded King Khalid, and he was accused by Iran as not being fit to be called Custodian of the two

Holy Mosques. This touched a raw nerve and he called an Islamic conference in order to gain support to isolate Iran and its extremist attitude.

King Fahad, mindful of the reputation of Saudis abroad living the high life, introduced a programme of personal austerity, which he extended throughout the royal household. Saudi nobility and the upper echelons of their society had been used, over the years, to spending the summer months away from the stifling heat, in the spas and resorts of the Mediterranean where stories of their high living and spending were legendary. Lesser ranks often headed east to the dubious areas of Bombay or Bangkok. A Royal decree ordered all Saudis to return home immediately.

Furthermore King Fahad advocated less lavish weddings and a significant reduction in dowry payments. None of these measures however stopped the flow of rhetoric from Iran. Another element now came into the picture. By 1985 Iraq's financial position was critical and Saudi Arabia was effectively funding the war against Iran.

The impact of the revolution in Iran affected all parts of the region in different ways. Old established trade routes and trade partners disappeared, so new avenues of business had to be established.

I know that this is going to sound somewhat trivial in view of the grave situation in the Gulf at the time, but new opportunities presented themselves to our company as a result.

Earlier, I mentioned an Iranian company, which was distributing a snack food product throughout the Gulf. This trade stopped abruptly after the revolution. One morning, I had a call from a packaging machine company in Uxbridge. I already knew my counterparts there and had a good rapport with them. An Indian gentleman had arrived there straight from Heathrow and was negotiating the purchase of a complete snack line, plus the packaging machines. He also wanted the Cellophane to run on them.

I drove to Uxbridge by early afternoon, and met Lalchand Valabdas. He was Indian but his factory, which he ran with his brother Mahesh, was in Dubai. So began a good commercial relationship, which meant regular visits to Dubai. The loss of the Iranian business was more than offset by this new market quickly followed by other operations in Bahrain, Dhahran, and Oman of which more later.

In the late 1970s, a chill wind was blowing through the British economy. Inflation under the Labour government was in double figures, and it took regular "beer and sandwich" meetings at Number 10 with the Trade Unions to resolve disputes over pay and conditions. For exporters it was a good time. Exchange rates were in our favour and we were competitive.

We had a new Sales Director, totally supportive of our team's efforts. I was still concentrating on my markets of Yemen and Iraq despite the war. Paul's areas too were equally successful. Ideally the company wanted a 75% UK 25% Export turnover, but with the UK market so flat they were only too happy to accept a higher export figure which at one time reached 40%.

The world was certainly a troubled place. The IRA had stepped up its bombing campaign and brought the terrorists attack to mainland Britain. Security at Heathrow now saw armed troops guarding all terminals. Hijackings were causing major problems, and security at all worldwide airports became a common feature.

My first experience of the new security regime came

at Frankfurt where I underwent a very physical search by a security officer. She was a very well built uniformed fraulein, and her inspection investigated parts of me, which hitherto, I had thought private and personal! At first I found it unacceptable, but soon realised how necessary it was. By complete contrast, security at Athens was non-existent, which I found worrying.

Travelling to Iraq became a problem. I went by bus from Amman to Baghdad and back when Iraqi airspace was closed. Then a limited air service operated from Amman and later Cyprus.

The signing of a treaty between Egypt and Israel provoked a furious reaction from other Arab countries. My travelling to war zones required special insurance cover but although the Middle East continued to attract negative headlines, I never felt in any personal danger.

So things may have been difficult in the UK, but it was a good time for exporters. The Treasury even gave export travellers a bonus by allowing us to reclaim income tax on periods working abroad above thirty days a year. This was later cancelled in by Chancellor Nigel Lawson, who accused us of having a good time abroad! I don't know what planet he was on but this was the start of the Thatcher years.

Chapter 13

The Road to Damascus

Having succeeded in establishing business in Iraq, Yemen, and Saudi Arabia, I was not fooled into thinking that developing the rest of the Middle East would necessarily be as straightforward.

Going to Syria during a trip in the early part of 1979 was to prove this. This revelation did not come in a blinding flash of light such as that which Saul of Tarsus experienced on the road to Damascus, but in a far more mundane fashion.

I was excited about going to Damascus, one of the world's oldest cities. The city had such a pivotal role to play in the spread of Christianity and I suppose is second only to Jerusalem, a city, which I could not visit. Israel refused to accept passports, which had visas of other Middle Eastern countries stamped in them. I know that some people did have a separate passport, fly to Cyprus, post their other passport home, then go to Israel. This all took time and was costly and our view was that there was not enough business available in Israel to justify this measure.

We wanted to see what opportunities there were for us in Syria, Egypt, and Jordan, so I added these countries to my itinerary.

Arriving in Damascus, my first impression was that it

had seen better days. Rather elegant buildings were looking tired and in need of restoration. Streets were not as busy as those in Baghdad. I was aware that Syria's economic position was poor compared with its neighbour Iraq. There was no oil revenue to bolster the Syrian economy and it did not attract the same level of foreign investment.

Syria was established as a country after World War 1. Then the whole region was carved up between the interests of France and Britain. It remained under a French mandate until it achieved full independence in 1946.

The political scene thereafter was marred by countless coups, and it was not until President Hafez Al Assad came to power in 1971 that any sort of stability was established. This stability came at a price in that emergency laws, which had been in place since 1962 were further strengthened by the ruling Baath Party leaving ordinary citizens with virtually no rights. It is against these laws that the present protests in Syria are being made and ruthlessly crushed by President Bashar Al Assad who succeeded his father.

There was fierce personal rivalry between Hafez Al Assad and Saddam Hussein. Each wanted to appear as the leader of Arab nationalism, and there were regular skirmishes of the border between Syria and Iraq. I found this rivalry a little strange because both countries middle classes were basically Sunni Muslims with a significant Christian presence. Many traders and businesses in Iraq had Syrian origins going back to the days when neither country existed as such. Both countries had a Baath Socialist party in power.

Talks on possible unification with Iraq were held in 1979 at a time when Syria needed all the allies it could get. Problems with its neighbours Lebanon, Israel and the activities of the PLO threatened to bring all out war. Negotiations stalled partly because of differences in the policies of the two Baath parties. Another reason was the fact that, although each country had Sunni and Shia Muslims, the Syrian government was made up largely from a third sect, the Alawis.

A quick look around the market area showed that there was not the quality of goods that there was in Iraq, which reflected on the spending power of the locals. I noticed that many products had been imported from Turkey.

We had a contact with a company, whose owner used to visit the UK once a year and do a tour of various printing companies buying any unwanted stocks of material at a knock down price. We were always careful to ensure that any material we sold him did not carry the name of any customer or a brand name.

I was taken to a printing factory, which I was told produced material for the local confectionery industry. The printing press, which was in operation, would have done credit to any of Heath Robinson's creations. Wooden print rollers were being driven by a system of chain pulleys. Rubber stereos were mounted on the rollers and ink was transferred from the surface of other rollers, which rotated in an ink duct.

What alarmed me most, was the sight of material with the name Cadbury's being overprinted with a local name. This material had not come from us but one of our competitors. I think I knew then that this was not going to be a market for me.

My hotel was in central Damascus and during the siesta hour I walked to the market area and the remnants of the old city. There I found Straight Street of Biblical fame. The large Roman arch at the entrance was very impressive and must have been here when Saul of Tarsus took refuge at a house in Straight Street after he was temporally blinded on the road to

Damascus where he had intended to carry on his persecution of the Jews.

The Bible records that a man called Ananias had a vision in which God told him to go to Straight Street and find the house of a man called Judas. There he would find Saul. Knowing Saul's reputation, Ananias was at first reluctant to go, but he obeys the command. At the house he lays his hands on Saul and his sight is restored. Ananias baptises Saul who thereafter is known as Paul.

Over the centuries, Straight Street must have seen many changes but the narrow confines of the buildings along its 1.500 metre length retain a unique atmosphere and I wished that I had had more time to explore it.

On the way back to the hotel, I came to a road intersection where traffic was negotiating a roundabout. As I watched as two flashy sports cars sped round and round it at great speed and then drove off along the road, obviously racing. A traffic policeman nearby seemed totally unconcerned at this behaviour. When I told my contact about this incident he explained that the drivers were almost certainly the sons of Government officials and they were allowed to get away with it.

I did venture back to Syria for one day in 1982 after hearing that a new regulation had been passed banning the use of imported packaging material with brand names on. However a visit to a couple of factories convinced me that it would take several years before this rule was observed because of high stock levels. Indeed one chocolate manufacturer told me that packaging material with a foreign brand name helped sell his product as people thought it was imported!

Other problems were affecting the Syrian economy at this time. Because of its proximity to Lebanon, there was no way it could avoid being affected by the bitter fighting in Beirut. Israel's fight with the Palestinian Liberation Army also threatened to spill over frequently into Syria. Beirut had for years been the banking centre used by most Damascus businessmen, but the closure of the Damascus road to Beirut by the Israelis caused major financial problems.

All in all Syria was not a place to hang around in. The PLO was openly using Syria as a base to attack Israel, and even in central Damascus I saw groups of heavily armed PLO militia walking around. Israel's response was to occupy the Golan Heights overlooking Syria's border, an area that was to see much fighting.

I had seen enough and did not return to this market again.

Chapter 14

Moses Place

1978/9 and I was expanding my search for suitable Middle East markets for our business. Some of our associate companies in Greece, Holland, France and Spain wanted to get involved in this export trade, and I was asked to look out for opportunities for them.

When planning my trips, I had to prepare a schedule giving details of what my aims were in a particular market or markets, how long I was going to be there, and how much it was all going to cost.

These details were entered on what was called "The Green Form" and submitted to the Sales and Managing Director for approval or otherwise. Nothing could be booked until this process had taken place.

I will confess though, that when travelling to other countries, I always thought that, if the opportunity came up to see some of the famous places there, I would take it.

In Iraq, I was incredibly lucky in that over a period of fifteen years, my travels took me to the far north and south of the country and I had the opportunity of seeing Babylon, Nineveh, Samarra, Kerbala, Hatra, and many other historic places. If normal conditions ever return to Iraq, these places will certainly be on the tourist trail.

So when I planned my first visit to Egypt, you won't be surprised if I wondered if I would have time to see the Pyramids and the Sphinx.

First things first though and the main object of the visit was to appoint an agent to represent our company. Mahmoud Rifaat was a large Egyptian, seemingly as wide as he was tall. He certainly knew the kind of business we were interested in and we set off on a whistle stop tour of the confectionery and biscuit manufacturers of Cairo. Speed was not an option. Cairo traffic was, and is, notoriously chaotic. It is every man, camel and donkey for themselves. I marvelled at how someone could drive a herd of goats the wrong way down a one way street through oncoming traffic. Add to that the noise of car horns, traffic sounds, and heavy pollution, and you will get some idea of what travelling around Cairo was like.

Mahmoud was used to all this and bulldozed his car through the morass of people, cars, buses, vans, lorries, all intermixed with goats, donkeys and camels to get to our destinations. He did not believe in walking anywhere. At one time he drove down an alleyway so narrow that had the car had to stop for any reason we would not have been able to open the doors. There can only have been a couple of inches clear on both sides. Also the surface underneath was very uneven because rubbish was disposed of by throwing it into the alley and passing traffic compressed it down.

Getting to one sweet company, we passed an area known as The City of the Dead. It is four miles long and is a confused maze of large tombs and elaborate mausoleums. In this place though, live many Egyptians who are either too poor to live anywhere else or who have been forced out of the slums in central Cairo to make way for other developments. There were also many migrants who had come from the countryside looking for work.

In the evening on my first day, Mahmoud took me for a meal at Cairo's Royal Automobile Club, a classical type building from the 1920s which was popular with the more affluent members of Egyptian society, and certainly looked that way on my visit. I was surprised that it was still called Royal in view of the abolition of the monarchy.

It was gone midnight when we emerged from the Club into a cold October night. As we stood waiting to get a taxi, I heard a baby's cry coming from a doorway next to us. It was so dark that I had a job making out where the noise came from, but as I looked more closely, I could see a woman dressed in black huddled on the floor. The baby must have been inside her clothing. The contrast between the place we had just come from and the place where this woman and child were spending the night could not have been greater. There was I going to a comfortable hotel room. There was nothing I could do, but the image has always stayed with me.

I was due to leave Cairo for Sanaa on a flight leaving at twenty past midnight. My last evening was free and with about three hours of daylight left, I decided to get a taxi and go to Giza to see the Pyramids and the Sphinx. The area was quiet. All the tourists had departed back to their hotels. A few camels and their owners were hanging around hoping for last minute customers, and I declined all bids to get me on one.

As I walked across the open sand to take some photographs, I was approached by a man, who asked me, if I would like to enter the Great Pyramid. It seemed like a good idea so I paid him the entrance fee, which wasn't very much. He led me to the entrance and into the pyramid.

I was instantly aware that I was going to have to watch my head. My guide said that I could see the burial chambers, the first of which could be reached by crawling through a shaft about thirty feet long as far as I can remember, but only about four feet high. So I scrabbled my way along noticing how sharply the temperature had dropped to a clammy cold. I came to a chamber rectangular in shape – empty of course!

I then had to crawl back, but there was more. My guide directed me to a long vertical staircase, which was extremely steep and got narrower at the top. It was a real effort to climb and I was very glad of the handrail on one side. By the time I got to the top my legs were aching. At the top a low entrance led into a chamber in the centre of which was a stone sarcophagus. The air in the chamber was cool but having seen it, I was now feeling somewhat claustrophobic, and was anxious to get out. This involved coming down the staircase backwards and very gingerly, and then out into the late evening sunlight. I thanked my guide and gave him a tip. There was hardly anyone around now. All the camels had gone, but as I looked across the open ground I could see a souvenir stall still open. Its title was "Moses Place"! This was the only reference to Moses that I saw.

The site of the Pyramids and the Sphinx in the desert area just outside Giza is impressive but I think I was more impressed by the inside of the Great Pyramid rather than the outside. The statistics and construction methods are really quite mind boggling. All measurements were designed to support the internal slabs of stone and prevent them collapsing into the burial chambers. The Great Pyramid, one of the original wonders of the world, was for 4000 years the highest building in the world. It took the building of the spire of Lincoln Cathedral in 1300 to claim the record at that time.

It is estimated that more than 2.3million stones were required and 200,000 workers. Without accurate measuring equipment, the four sides at the base are accurate to an error of only two inches. I could not help but marvel at the sight and felt very privileged to have been inside the Pyramid.

I did get the chance on a later visit to Cairo to visit the National Museum where many of the artefacts are now displayed. The building is very old fashioned and the exhibits and their cases looked as if they could do with a good dusting. However the gold masks, statues, sculptures, and drawings are all reminders of a great ancient empire. Hopefully they have survived the recent turmoil in the Egyptian uprising.

The story of Moses leading the people of Israel out of Egypt occupies the Book of Exodus. Some cynics say that Moses made a grave error after he had crossed the Red Sea, and that he should have turned right instead of left!

The fact is that Moses, after many trials and tribulations, led his people to within sight of The Promised Land, which he was destined not to set foot in.

What is now modern day Jordan was to be the nearest that Moses got to The Promised Land. He was to see it from the top of Mount Nebo, and shortly afterwards he died.

I had an unexpected chance to take in the same view whilst on a visit to Jordan in the early 1980s. I was due to leave on an early morning KLM flight to Amsterdam. Queen Alia airport is a good forty five minutes south of Amman and I arrived in good time at around 5.30am. I checked in, in the normal way, unaware of any problems. The flight was due to take off at 7.30am but as that time approached, there was no sign of us boarding the aircraft. Then we were told there would be a short delay. This stretched into a couple of hours and we were then informed that due to a technical fault, the flight would not be leaving until at least 6.00pm.

The flight would not have been full by any means and

there were probably only about eighty passengers waiting. A KLM representative offered to take us back to Amman to rest in a hotel, have a meal, and then those who wished could go on a coach trip to the Dead Sea. Needless to say I wasn't going to pass up that opportunity.

As in Egypt, land away from the River Jordan valley is fairly barren but has a beauty all of its own. Our route took us west up into the hills. The air was clear and visibility was perfect as we stopped for a while on Mount Nebo in view of "The Promised Land".

In the middle distance, the Dead Sea shimmered in the sunlight whilst in the far distance was the outline of Jerusalem with the sun reflecting on the golden Dome of the Rock.

Then it was down to the shore of the Dead Sea, and as I sat at a table outside a café with a cold drink, I watched the bathers floating in the salt water where they say it is impossible to sink.

The Book of Deuteronomy records that:

Moses went up from the plains of Moab to Mount Nebo. The Lord said to Moses, "I have let you see it but I will not let you go there." So Moses, the Lord's servant, died there in the land of Moab as the Lord said he would.

Poor Moses. Life's not always fair is it?

Chapter 15

Foreigners Forbidden

In the early 1980s it was the war between Iraq and Iran, which dominated the Middle East news. It showed no sign of any early conclusion, and Kuwait in particular was very apprehensive about the fighting going on just across its border. Many businesses had curtailed operations and a steady flow of migrant workers was leaving the country for fear of the conflict spilling over into Kuwait.

From being a country, which welcomed Heads of State in the 1970s, including Queen Elizabeth in 1979, the Kuwaiti Royal Family now found itself under threat. An attempt was made on the Emir's life. The American embassy was damaged by a bomb. As a result Kuwait frequently closed its borders and a complete screening process took place on all non-Kuwaitis resident in the country. Anyone with Iranian connections was immediately deported. There was also a suspicion that some members of the Iraqi Shia community were siding with the Iranians, so similar restrictions were imposed, and no visas were granted to Iraqis even though Kuwait fully supported Iraq in the war. As the Iranians advanced into the Faw Peninsula the sound of gunfire could clearly be heard in Kuwait City.

Further tension was added in 1980 when the Americans attempted a rescue mission in Teheran to free fifty two hostages. The attempt went badly wrong, and had to be abandoned leaving eight servicemen dead. Meanwhile in London, the SAS successfully stormed the Iranian Embassy where nineteen hostages had been held for six days.

1981 saw race riots in several cities in the UK, including Bristol. In the Middle East, President Sadat of Egypt was assassinated and replaced by Hosni Mobarak. The British Prime Minister, Margaret Thatcher was hell bent on confronting the Trade Unions, and trouble was brewing. To lighten the general gloom, the country celebrated the marriage of Prince Charles and Lady Diana Spencer. Also Botham and Willis destroyed the Aussies to gain an Ashes test victory.

Attention was diverted away from domestic strife in 1982, when the Falklands were invaded by the Argentinians. The victorious war that followed was short and bloody. Diplomacy failed utterly.

The Leader of the PLO, Yasser Arafat was forced out of Beirut and members of the PLO scattered and fled to Syria, Jordan, Yemen, Sudan and Tunisia. There then followed a horrific period of ethnic cleansing of Palestinian refugees in the camps of Chatila and Sabra.

In this country there was outcry at the plans to allow the USA to store nuclear missiles at UK bases.

I tell you all this because in a troubled world, trying to put together a viable export programme was getting harder and harder.

Flights into Iraq had resumed, but only from Amman, and then only at night with fighter escorts. The runway lights at Saddam International Airport were switched on only as the aircraft approached for its final landing.

Business in Iraq however was continuing as were many projects in Saudi Arabia and the Gulf.

I was now travelling to the region four times a year with each visit lasting fifteen to twenty days. Looking back at my flight schedules, I was averaging eleven flights a trip, going from Muscat in the south to Mosul in the north, and many places in between. Flights operated by Gulf Air, Saudia, and Kuwait Air had become far more frequent as demand had grown, and it was now far easier to plan a time effective trip. I could work in say Dubai for a couple of days, catch an evening flight and start work next day in Bahrain. Flights into Yemen were also improving, and instead of having to allow four days I could now make a visit in two.

Trips were becoming routine. Established customers were used to me turning up regularly, and new businesses were opening up as food production in the region continued to expand.

In Saudi Arabia, I was now going to Riyadh and Dhahran, as well as Jeddah. Saudi authorities were still somewhat nervous about foreigners criss-crossing the Kingdom, and visa applications had to be accompanied by letters of invitation from Saudi companies before a visa was granted to travel within the Kingdom.

Several companies were now producing the corn curl snack product previously made in Iran. Maize meal was imported from Italy, and on visits to factories I could see that storage facilities were not good especially with the heat and humidity. Infestation by weevils was commonplace and I did not think too hard about what was being fed into the hoppers of the extruding machines!

Although Jeddah, Riyadh, and Dhahran were the main areas, I did get to visit a couple of out of the way places. The first was Hofuf, a half hour flight from Dhahran. This was a small town in the east. Apart from the fact that it was near a large oil drilling area, there was nothing of note about the place. My customer was producing snack foods hoping to get a contract to supply the oil installation.

The second was far more interesting and required special clearance from the Saudi Embassy. We had supplied packaging to a new company in Medina, and the owner, Hussein Hajjar had requested me to visit him. Technically, Medina, the second most holy city after Mecca, is off limits to non-Muslims.

The factory had been built on a new industrial site to the north of the city, whereas the airport was on the southern side. Mr Hajjar sent me a letter of invitation, and I was granted permission, recorded in my visa, to go provided Mr Hajjar met me at Medina airport and returned me there after my visit. I had to present the visa at Jeddah airport before they would let me board the plane.

As we flew northwards, I had a clear view of the terrain below. On the sands I could often see the tracks left by camels. Passing over a series of mountains, I noticed that there were craters in some with black lava still visible, a reminder that this area at one time was volcanic.

At Medina airport, a security official studied the visa, and then took me into the Arrival's Hall where Mr Hajjar was waiting. Having handed me over to him, we then drove through the centre of the city, on what must have been a dedicated through road towards the industrial estate. At each road intersection on the right and left were large signs in Arabic and English reading FOREIGNERS FORBIDDEN.

On the way, there was a call to prayer, and Mr Hajjar got out of the car and prayed on a mat by the side of the road for ten minutes. After the return journey to the airport, Mr Hajjar handed me over to a security official who shepherded me through to the departure gate. All in all, it was a weird experience.

Around this time, I paid my first visit to Oman. It had been just over ten years since this country formerly known as The Sultanate of Muscat & Oman had been transformed into a modern developing state simply called Oman. The inspiration and driving force behind this change was Sultan Qaboos.

Prior to 1970, life was primitive in the extreme. The country was ruled by Sultan Qaboos' father, Sultan Saud bin Taymur. He was an absolute monarch, and nothing could be done without his approval. He rejected any diplomatic relations with other countries. He forbade the use of radios. In the city of Muscat, a curfew operated after dark, and anyone outside the city walls without a lantern could be shot. Medical care was confined to one under equipped hospital, and only two schools existed in the whole country.

Sultan Qaboos had been educated abroad and had trained at Sandhurst Military Academy. Horrified by the way his father was running the country, he forced his father to abdicate, and a new era came into being.

Sultan Qaboos bin Said issued a promise to the nation on the July 23rd 1970. He stated that he would introduce immediately a programme of reform, education, and regeneration. Exiles were encouraged to return to Oman to spearhead all the changes. A Government was formed, and diplomatic relations established with all neighbouring countries. By 1975, over 260 schools had been built.

My first visit was in April 1980. I took a direct flight from Heathrow and landed at Seeb airport at twenty past midnight. Immigration and customs clearance was surprisingly quick compared with other Middle East airports. At that time Seeb airport was small and going outside the terminal, trying to find a taxi proved problematic. This puzzled me as airports normally are well served by taxis. When eventually one came, we set off and in the darkness, I quickly realised that we were travelling along a dirt road. I was unaware that Muscat is some twenty miles away from Seeb airport, and it was not until we reached the outskirts of Muscat that we met a paved road.

I was staying in a small hotel, and next morning, as dawn broke, I could see that we were overlooking a long *corniche* encompassing the harbour. Fishing boats were bringing in the early morning's catch. I went out for a stroll to see what they had caught and there were some very odd looking specimens. Just outside the harbour, at anchor, were several large oil tankers. Muscat had now become a prime loading terminal as owners were reluctant to send vessels further up the Gulf because of the Iraq/Iran war.

My reason for coming to Oman was to meet Ali Shaihani or to give him his full name Ali Khudadat Ahmed Al Shaihani. I think he must have been one of the exiles who returned to Oman. He too had been a distributor of the Iranian corn curl product, and was now completing a factory to make the corn curls himself. We had already supplied him with material for freeze pops being made in an adjoining soft drinks factory, which had been opened a couple of years earlier. Both factories were on land, which had been created for an industrial site by literally removing a hill.

Ali Shaihani is one of those larger than life characters. He was running both operations with military precision. His office was like a command post. All operatives in the factories had been given two way radios, and our negotiations were constantly interrupted by messages coming in, and his instructions going out, but a deal was done.

It was a pleasure doing business with Ali Shaihani, and once he had gone into production, he sent drivers out with vans loaded with product to hand out free samples in the city markets and schools as well as in the surrounding villages. An instant demand was created, and so successful was the operation, that he ordered a second extruder and packaging machine, and doubled our order.

I also went to the commercial section of the British Embassy, which was located at the far end of the *corniche*. It was in an old fort, and its grounds led down to the sea where I noticed a small yacht was moored. I was told that it had been requested that they move to a new diplomatic area on the edge of the city, but this suggestion was being resisted. The Commercial Attache wasn't any help and seemed only interested in public sector projects of which there were many.

On a later visit to Oman a couple of years later, I went to an industrial area fairly near Seeb airport, now well served by paved roads. On the way I noticed that every 100 yards or so, marker poles were on either side of the road. I asked the driver what these were, and he told me that the area was subject to flash flooding at certain times of the year. I thought this rather odd but he said that the rain fell in the mountains, and with the ground being rocky, the water rushed down the mountainsides into the valleys and then out into the open plain on its way to the sea.

Demonstrating the force that could be created by these inland rainstorms was an incident in which a block of flats next to one of Ali Shaihani's factories was washed away by a wall of water which came from a valley immediately behind the industrial estate. Several of his workers were killed as a result.

Oman was, in a way, the final piece of the jigsaw of

the food operations filling the gap left by the withdrawal of the Iranian product. However new problems arose because manufacturers were complaining that their local markets were being infiltrated by product from neighbouring countries and as a result a price war developed.

In Bahrain, the situation was even more chaotic. No fewer than three manufacturers were competing with each other for what was a small market. We produced some packaging for one of them depicting cartoon characters. I found out later that children bought the packs only for the designs, and threw away the product!

I did not ignore Iraq at this difficult time for them. After a sixteen hour bus ride from Amman there and back, I was then able to get flights when they resumed from Amman and business continued to come our way.

All in all, things were going well.

Chapter 16

Letters from Far Off Places

As I sit typing this narrative on my computer, I cannot help but marvel at the technology, which enables me to make contact with people anywhere in the world, more or less, at the touch of a button.

I am a recent convert to the internet and e-mail facility. I do have a mobile phone, which is usually switched off, and which I use very infrequently. However I recognise that I am in the minority here, for when I am out and about, every other person seems to be talking or texting on one. I don't blog or tweet and am not even sure what those terms mean.

The latest mobile phones allow the user to do all manner of things, too numerous to list and I cannot help thinking that someone in silicone valley is hard at work designing the next "must have" gizmo and probably the one after that as well. There is a veritable fruit salad out there. How long before Blackberries, Apples and Oranges are joined by Cherries, Pears and Grapefruit?

Turn the clock back thirty or more years and none of these things existed and were the stuff of science fiction. When I went off to the Middle East in the mid 1970s, the only way I could let my wife, Ve, know that I had arrived safely was to send a cable. By the early 1980s hotels and some companies had installed a telex facility so I was able to send a message to the office, and my boss Paul, bless him, would telephone Ve to let her know I was OK.

By the mid 1980s, international dialling was in place, and this made things much easier. So in the ten years before these improvements in communications were available, the only way I could give my wife a picture of what I was up to, was to write letters. Airmail was surprisingly quick, and my letters usually arrived three days after sending them.

The following are some extracts from those letters.

From Baghdad: We went to see a new customer today. He didn't speak any English except he kept calling me "my dear". I didn't get too close! I've had the usual vast amount of tea, water, thick black Turkish coffee, and Pepsi. I've sampled local cheese [ugh] and manna [nice].

From Baghdad: On arrival at Baghdad airport, I thought Customs were going to be fussy because they seemed to be searching everyone's luggage very thoroughly. There was an Arab woman in front of me and they took everything out of her cases, and dumped it on the side. When it came to my turn the officer looked at me and said "Breeetish" and when I nodded he chalked my case without opening it!

From Kuwait: I must say it's nice to get to a decent hotel and get a hot bath. The flight from Dhahran was on time yesterday, but when we got to Kuwait airport, an Iranair jumbo jet had landed before us and there were about 70 Iranian workers in front of each of the immigration desks. They all appeared to be illiterate as none had filled in the landing cards, so security officers were having to fill them in as they went through. After

½ hour it became obvious that they were processing them at the rate of 4 per hour. I went with a couple of Americans and persuaded a security officer to let us through otherwise we would have been there all day.

From Cairo: I've been down the dark alleys of Cairo amongst the sweet makers, drinking innumerable cups of thick black coffee and sucking lots of boiled sweets. These alleys get dirtier every time I see them. All refuse is simply thrown into the street and it gets trodden under foot with the ruts getting deeper. The agent insists on driving down these alleys. He is a large fat man who doesn't like walking anywhere. We must look exact opposites, a bit like Laurel and Hardy.

From Taiz: There were five foreigners on the plane. Apart from me there was a French man, a Vietnamese woman, a Japanese man and his wife. We decided to share a taxi into Taiz, and knowing the usual arguments, decided we wouldn't pay any more than 20 rials each, about £2. We were approached by a man, who obviously organised the taxis, and he said he wanted 200 rials, so we said no. He gradually brought the figure down and stuck on 120 rials and we still said no. He got quite upset and obviously passed the word around that 120 rials was the asking rate and that no one should accept less. For a time there was a stand off, then one of the taxi drivers said 100 rials and much to the supervisor's annoyance, we jumped in and off we went.

From Sanaa: I've got to Sanaa, but not by plane. Yemenair cancelled my flight this morning as they had too many pilgrims to take to Jeddah. So I've had to come up by road this afternoon. I didn't mind too much. Even though I've done the trip 5 times before by road, I still enjoy the views. Our only problem was trying to keep ahead of an electric storm. We could see it coming over the mountains to the west. There was no thunder but vivid blue flashes, which got even more dramatic as darkness fell. We reached Sanaa at 6 o'clock and I've been watching the lightening over the mountains.

From Baghdad: I've been to the Ghassan's for lunch, masgouf fish, lamb and rice in large quantities. These Friday lunches are always family occasions. Mr & Mrs Ghassan, Hicham [Ghassan's brother] and his wife who is Ghassan's wife's sister, Ghassan's daughter, Hicham's two sons Beshar 20 and Zaid 15 plus Uncle Jacob and lastly their mother-in-law, so it was quite a crowd. I was kept busy with my camera.

From Dhahran: Another new customer today. This man is in his mid twenties and is getting married in a fortnight's time. On our way back from his factory, we stopped at a furniture store because he had to settle the colour of the bedroom suite. He asked me to have a look at it. I doubt they've got anything like it even in Harrod's. Everything was covered in blue velvet with a gold metallic finish even down to the bedside fridge. The bed was at least 7ft across with an enormous headboard, which contained a stereo music centre and a remote control to alter the angle of the mattress. The price was 17000 Saudi Riyals equivalent to £2360.

From Baghdad: On the flight from Belgrade, we stopped briefly at Damascus. There was a woman with a baby girl about 6 months old, sitting next to me. The baby was getting fractious so she was handed to me whilst the mother went off to get some hot water to make a feed. I think the shock of being dumped on a total stranger was enough to keep baby quiet until mother got back.

From Istanbul: The petrol problem is quite something and has been the focal point all day. First of all, the agent should have been here at 9am and turned up at 10am full of apologies because his car had run out of petrol and he had had to leave it. He reckons he will have to queue for 6 hours tonight before he can get any. So we have been everywhere by taxi and the arguing point is not how much it will cost but whether or not there is enough petrol in the tank to get us there. One other snag is that some unscrupulous garages are mixing water in with the petrol. This floats on top and gives a false reading on the fuel gauge. We were in one taxi where the fuel gauge showed ¼ full when the car stopped right in the middle of a bridge. Amidst much hooting and tooting, we pushed the car to the side of the road and had to leave it there.

From Cairo: I got an order from a new customer today after 3½ hours of haggling. During the "discussions" he got a mirror out of his desk drawer and leant it against a calendar. Then he got some shaving soap, lathered himself and had a shave. All this time he continued to haggle. After that, he pulled out a parcel wrapped in newspaper and out came a pie which he broke into three pieces and handed us a piece each. All morning we had been supplied with 7up, Cola, tea and coffee so after 3½ hours I was absolutely busting. As we were in quite a modern office I felt sure that they would have a loo, so I politely enquired. The customer said yes but would I wait a few minutes. He summoned a minnion who departed at great speed. About ten minutes later he came back, and took me down a flight of stairs to a small room where there was a line of ground level basins, obviously the factory communal loo. He cleared everyone out and stood guard outside whilst I was inside.

From Baghdad: Thursday afternoons and evenings are the peak times for weddings and there have been quite a few today. Cars, lorries and pick-ups all bedecked in ribbons have been tearing up and down with horns blaring for several hours. Some of the lorries have bands playing whilst others carry wedding cakes which can be anything from 13 to 19 tiers high. Usually two or three men stand by the cake to make sure it doesn't topple over.

From Cairo: My flight was on time. The plane was full of a party of Americans on a "Discover the Treasures of Egypt" package tour, so you can guess they were well armed with guides and maps. The noise level of conversation was quite overpowering. My agent met me and I was given V.I P. treatment and whisked through Immigration and Customs in minutes. His brother is the Airport Manager. Our taxi driver seemed affected by the extremely hot weather. He kept taking his hands off the steering wheel, putting them to his face and saying "Cairo no good, Cairo no good."

From Baghdad: As usual there are delegations from other countries in Baghdad, the main one being from Turkey. At the end of the road is a platform with the Iraqi and Turkish flags on. There is a delegation from Pakistan coming tomorrow and they are busy taking the Turkish flags down and putting the Pakistan ones up. I wonder if they ever get them mixed up. We were down in the Shorja market today and "Sunday lunch" consisted of greasy grilled chicken and flat bread washed down by something like strong Ribena. It was so strong it made my voice go funny for about two hours.

We had dinner tonight in a restaurant where they had a cabaret. There was quite a good band but Top of the Bill was a belly dancer. She was a hefty wench and certainly did wonders for the locals. Not my type though and it's not old age! The act was like a frenzied version of the Hokey Cokey. She put a lot out and in and shook a lot more than the British version. All very educational!

From Cairo: Originally we were going to Alexandria by train like we did last time. The agent couldn't get seats so we had to go by road. I can see why he prefers to go by train and frankly I would refuse to go by road again. The road is dual carriageway, dead straight and flat for 120 miles. It is also liberally sprinkled with potholes and debris, which is thrown up and hits the cars. The main risk is from huge lorries with long trailers, illegal in the UK. They thunder up and down at incredible speeds. Every few miles you can see the result of an accident with the wreckage left at the side of the road. The most spectacular happened just a few minutes before we arrived on the scene. A timber lorry had parted company with its rear wheels, which had wrapped themselves around a telegraph pole. The lorry had gone on a further 50 yards before crashing into a tree scattering planks of wood all over the road. Mercifully the driver appeared to be uninjured.

I spent the whole day in a biscuit factory, which was not air conditioned. It was very dirty and had the most enormous cockroaches and many other insects, so I sampled as few of the products as was polite! They insisted on taking us to lunch at a "Family Restaurant", which was filthy even by Egyptian standards. Before we got there, we got caught up in the most monumental traffic jam. They have introduced traffic lights in the area about a week ago but no one takes any notice of them. So at a crossroads, four lines of traffic had met head on and we could not move forwards or backwards, with traffic building up behind us. For 1½ hours we were stuck in this lot with everyone shouting, fist waving, horn blowing and spitting, but no actual blows were struck. Eventually, two policemen managed to divert some cars onto some waste ground, which created enough space to get traffic moving again so we didn't have lunch until 4 o'clock. The less said about the lunch the better but I'm glad I've got my pink pills!

From Dhahran: I do get lumbered with some odd fellow passengers. From Medina to Tabuk, which is a military base, I had two Arabs next to me who hadn't flown before, at least, judging by the look of sheer terror on their faces when we took off, I don't think they had. I had to help them with their seat belts and when, during the flight, we were given orange juice in paper cups, they passed the empty cups to me and indicated to me to throw them out of the window!

From Cairo: The flight out [from Kuwait] was on time and uneventful except for an Egyptian with three wives. They could not get seats together and kicked up a terrible fuss. The plane was actually taxiing out on the runway before a stewardess persuaded them to sit in separate seats.

At 5.30pm we went to the old part of Cairo where "sweetmakers" have their factories. Most of the sweets are wrapped by hand using casual labour and very young children. To get there, I had to go down a maze of alleys, crowded with people, cats, goats and donkey carts. At the first place we sat around a desk surrounded by boxes of sugar and essences and negotiated by the light of a 40 watt light. By the time we finished it was pitch black outside with only a few dim lights in the alleys. Overall there was the smell of chocolate, toffee and the occasional whiff of urine.

From Baghdad: I was in one factory today and was asked to go into the office. It was filthy with bits of sweets all over the place. Then I saw an empty mousetrap on the desk. Yes, I was given sweets to eat!

Of course the correspondence was not one-way traffic. My wife Ve wrote to me as well and she would send letters to the next destination on my route so as to be there when I arrived. Usually this was successful and getting news from home always gave me a lift.

Chapter 17

No Room at the In[tercontinental]

The late 1970s were boom times for airlines and hotels, as business people from all over Europe flocked to the Middle East to tap into the new found prosperity of the region. The big European and American hotel chains had, by the early 1980s, built hotels in all the major cities, and most travellers had "loyalty" cards from Groups such as Holiday Inn, Intercontinental, Marriot, Hilton, Novotel and Meridian.

The on-going war between Iraq and Iran meant that by the early 1980s, the situation for travellers to the area had changed in that, instead of having problems getting flights or a hotel room, airlines and hotels were now chasing them for business. I had had to get clearance from Courtaulds to go to the Gulf, and special war cover insurance was arranged.

Most of the hotel groups had reservation offices in London, and for the first three destinations in Muscat, Dubai, and Bahrain I had booked with Intercontinental. I knew that the hotel in Manama, the capital of Bahrain, was a new one and I was curious to see what it was like.

At the best of times I am not the world's smartest dresser, and there's nothing like travelling in the Middle East in a jacket and tie etc. to give you that boiled lobster look. I always travelled light therefore, no jacket or tie. After the flight to

Bahrain, and grinding through immigration and customs, the only thing I wanted to do was to get to the hotel, have a shower, and a change of clothes.

Imagine my dismay therefore when I asked the taxi driver to take me to the Intercontinental when he said "Ees no open". Nevertheless I asked him to take me there. The ride took only ten minutes, and sure enough when we got there the place seemed deserted. I observed that there was only one car in the car park.

On the side of the building, I saw a man polishing a window. The taxi driver, who was still with me, asked him if the hotel was open, and he shook his head. A few yards along I came to what was going to be the main entrance, but there was still no sign of life. I was determined to find someone who could give me some information. I had a confirmed reservation, and I wanted to see if they had transferred me elsewhere.

I was about to give up and get back into the taxi, when a man rushed through the doors of the main entrance and down the imposing steps. By this time, I was dripping with sweat, but the man, dressed in a smart brown uniform, grabbed me by the hand, and shepherded me into the hotel. In the very large foyer I found myself being greeted on all sides by the General Manager, his Deputy, the Receptionists, Chefs, Waiters, Cleaners, and the Heads of all departments.

It appeared that it was opening day, and I was the first guest in this 384 room hotel. Far from being able to go and have a shower and a change of clothing, dishevelled as I was, I had to have a conducted tour of the whole building, and then be interviewed by a reporter from the *Gulf Mirror*.

Instead of an ordinary room, I was given a suite and all meals were to be "on the house". The next guest did not arrive until five hours later, so every time I left the room I was greeted with "Hello Mr. Freeman" by the Philippino staff, who seemed delighted to have a real live guest to practise on. One strange coincidence was that the General Manager was English and was born in Bristol.

I will never launch a ship, but I did launch a hotel!

Chapter 18

Like a Diamond in the Sky

Twinkle, twinkle little star,
How I wonder what you are.
Up above the world so high,
Like a diamond in the sky.

There can probably be no young child, or adult for that matter, that doesn't know the words and tune of this nursery rhyme. It is one of the first, if not the first, rhyme and tune that a youngster learns and performs to proud parents, grandparents, aunts, uncles etc.

What you probably don't know, and I didn't until I researched it, is that the tune is French, and the poem was written by a poetess, Jane Taylor in 1806 when she was just twenty-three. Sadly she died at the early age of forty in 1824.

It was whilst hearing the tune on a baby monitor when I was "baby sitting" for one of our granddaughters, that I was reminded of an odd event that happened in the early 1980s.

I have already mentioned my contact with Lalchand Valabdas from Dubai in an earlier chapter. He and his brother Mahesh were now running a very successful snack food company. They had had the advantage of being the first producer in the area and were selling not only in Dubai but throughout the whole Gulf region.

The two brothers were so pleasant to deal with. Not that they were a soft touch when it came to negotiations on price, but always accepted that in order to get a decent service and quality, their supplier needed to make a decent profit.

On one visit to Dubai, I was invited by Lalchand for a meal at his house with his family. As soon as I entered the house, I knew what was on the menu. Now I don't mind a mild curry, but it was no surprise that this curry was going to be hot, hot, hot! Much to the amusement of all, I worked my way through it, eating chapatis and drinking copious amounts of ice cold water.

On my next visit, the hotel I was staying in had recently opened a new restaurant and was advertising a curry night. Lalchand and Mahesh asked me to join them for a meal, and I had visions of another sizzling experience. However a cunning plan saved me, much to Lalchand and Mahesh's puzzlement. I had a quiet word with the restaurant manager before they arrived, and asked him to ensure that my curry was the mildest they could create, but to say nothing to Lalchand and Mahesh. The chef duly obliged and although I was aware they were watching me, I appeared to be consuming the same hot curry that they were. I did not let on what I had done!

If you are wondering what on earth all this has to do with the nursery rhyme, then please bear with me and I hope you will see the connection.

A few weeks later I heard from Lalchand that he was coming to London on business and would be contacting me. When he did telephone me he was in a state of panic. He had travelled on a British Airways flight direct from Dubai. He had, as his hand luggage, a black rectangular briefcase in which were not only his business papers, but also some diamonds which he intended to sell in London.

Imagine his consternation therefore, when halfway through the flight he opened the case to look at his business papers only to find that the briefcase contained someone else's papers. Somehow after the baggage screening process in Dubai, he or someone else had picked up the wrong briefcase. So where was his?

The cabin staff on his flight had acted very quickly when he alerted them to the problem. The captain radioed back to Dubai to see if there was any news of the missing briefcase. Sure enough a message had been received from another British Airways flight, which was on its way to Kuwait when one of its passengers had experienced the same problem.

The question now was how to reunite Lalchand with his property. At Heathrow BA staff had retained the briefcase which Lalchand had, and he had been informed that his would be on the next BA flight from Kuwait the following morning. He was told to come to Heathrow in the afternoon to collect it but he would need someone to vouch for him. I was only too happy to help and went and picked him up from his hotel near Heathrow. He certainly would have stood out in a crowd. A short man, he was wearing a vivid green and black striped blazer and a flat cap. His outfit seemed more suited to the Henley Regatta.

We duly contacted the BA desk in the terminal, and a member of staff took us through the Arrivals Hall via immigration and customs. Here Lalchand was reunited with his briefcase, and after the customs officer had inspected his diamonds paperwork, we were taken back through. The BA people were really helpful.

As I have already mentioned, the experience of working with Lalchand and his brother Mahesh was one of the best

I had during all the time I was travelling. I was even invited to Lalchand's daughter's wedding in India, but was unable to attend due to work commitments.

There is a sad end to this chapter however as in 1988 the two brothers were on Indian Airlines Flight 113 to Ahmedabad. The aircraft crashed on its approach to the airport and all 127 passengers were killed. It was a sad loss of two fine gentlemen.

Their company has survived and is still trading today. After the tragedy, other family members took control but I was never able to strike up the same relationship with them.

Chapter 19

It is the unforeseen that always happens

19TH CENTURY

"Expect the unexpected" was the advice given to me by Mr Toby in the early days of my exporting career. The trouble is that when things are going well, it was easy to become complacent and give no thought to possible problems ahead. I was certainly guilty of this.

From 1980 to 1985 the world was, as ever, in a state of turmoil. The Iraq/Iran war was assuming the trench-war status of the First World War with no possible solution in sight. The UK had fought and won a war against Argentina over the Falkland Islands. The Soviet Union was embarking on significant changes with the arrival of Mikhail Gorbachev.

My exporting schedules however were giving me no headaches. The snack food factories in the Gulf States were now fully operational, and happy to work on a twelve month contract basis. We were shipping container loads a month, and it needed only one visit a year from me.

Iraq in the meantime, regardless of the war, was yielding huge quantities of business amounting to around £4 million a year by 1985. I was now dealing with sixty companies and travelling not only to Baghdad but also Mosul, Kirkuk, Arbil, Kut, Kerbala and Musayib. The Iraq Government was still encouraging the production of all kinds of foodstuffs and our customers had no problems in obtaining import licences. Much of their production was earmarked for the army but it was deemed essential to maintain the country's morale by supplying the domestic market as well.

There was a slight hint that things might change when in 1985 licences for non-essential goods were not issued. Our packaging was not included, and I thought no more about it. Because of the increasing number of customers, I was spending more and more time in Iraq.

What was not expected was a dramatic fall in the price of oil early in 1986. At one time it had fallen to $20 a barrel. Iraq was entirely dependent on its oil revenue to fund the war. Iran's oil revenue had been more or less stopped because the loading ports in the Gulf had been put out of action. Iraq, on the other hand, was still able to pump oil through its pipeline via Turkey, and a second pipeline was nearing completion through Saudi Arabia.

With Iraq's finances now stretched to the limit, all new import licences were held back. Our customers were reassured that the measure was only temporary, and that the crisis over the price of oil would not last long. I didn't think it would last long either, but that was just wishful thinking as it turned out.

We had a new Managing Director at the time and having read my report from my visit to Iraq in April 1986, formed a very different view to mine. He was concerned that the company's export business was far too exposed in Iraq and that an urgent Plan B was required.

My boss, Paul, was about to retire. His markets had shrunk somewhat, and his Nigerian business was now being produced in our factory there. Other African business was being handled by a factory in Zimbabwe. I argued strenuously that the Iraq problem was only temporary, and that I needed to devote as much time as possible to maintaining the good relations built up with our customers.

The MD was not convinced, and with hindsight, rightly so. I was asked [not ordered] to do a market survey of the Indian sub-continent. Paul had visited India briefly a couple of years earlier and thought that there was potential there.

I was not at all happy about this turn of events. I felt that I had enough on my plate already, and in the eleven years I had been working in the Middle East, enough business had been generated and was still growing. A network of contacts among the European packaging machine suppliers and also ingredient suppliers, regularly meant that we were first on the scene when it came to supplying the packaging.

"But" I hear you say, "if you had been offered the chance to explore the Indian sub continent eleven years ago, you would have jumped at the chance". You would be quite right, I would have.

I suppose I had become "comfortable" working in the Middle East. I felt at ease there. I liked the people and got on well with them. I enjoyed their food or most of it. In some companies I had become more than a supplier and was regarded as a family friend by the owners and welcomed into their homes. None of this did I want to jeopardise, for loyalty is a two way virtue.

So it was a real dilemma and like all the big decisions in my life, I talked it over with my wife, Ve. Our family was growing up, our youngest was nine. With four trips a year, I was already away for what amounted to three months of the year leaving Ve to cope. I had no doubts that she could manage for she was a very strong and gifted character, but was it fair?

After much soul searching I said I would try and reach a

compromise with the company. I would do the trip as a one-off and if the results did offer significant potential, I would insist on them employing someone else to take it on full-time.

As things turned out, it was Saddam Hussein who solved the problem for me, although I was not to know that at the time.

I had little information to go on. Officially we had an agent in Sri Lanka, although we never heard from him. He was BCL's agent and, as in some other areas, we had appointed him as well. Fifteen years ago we had supplied a biscuit factory but nothing since. In India and Pakistan we had no agents.

I had a contact with a company in London who I knew had dealings not only with the area but also with Indonesia and the Philippines. They were willing to help and set up contacts for me in each of the countries.

I worked out a 21 day schedule starting in Colombo going on to Bombay [now Mumbai] and then Karachi and Lahore. On Saturday June 28th, I left Heathrow on BA 035 at 21.20am. This was a non-stop flight to Colombo arriving at 15.25am on Sunday afternoon. Because of the length of the flight, I was allowed to travel business class, which was nice.

Colombo airport, at Negombo, is some fifteen miles from the capital. Adjacent to the airport complex are many factories, many making clothing for export to High Street stores in the UK and Europe. The taxi ride to Colombo was a real eye opener. Firstly, I was struck by the vivid colours, not only of the lush vegetation but also of the bright colours of the clothes people were wearing. On either side of the road, was a mixture of dwellings and small shops, and I even spotted one with the unlikely name of Tesco!

Approaching the centre of Colombo, traffic increased,

and our one-hour journey was completed with the taxi weaving in and out of lorries, vans, and most of all, the motorised rickshaws known locally as "tuc tucs" because of the noise they make.

At last we reached the Lanka Oberoi, probably the nicest hotel I've ever stayed in. Rooms had a great outlook over the surrounding area, and mine looked out over some gardens and a lake towards a temple. The hotel was built in a rectangular shape with a huge covered atrium in the middle, which was used as a meeting place for guests. In the evenings, a small orchestra played classical and popular tunes. The acoustics were superb and made listening very enjoyable.

I had arranged a meeting that evening with our official agent. He was a pleasant enough fellow and was rather sheepish when I asked why we weren't getting any enquiries from him. He told me that his best customer was a local printing company, and that if he directed business our way, he might lose his unprinted film business with them. We agreed that this was an impossible situation for both of us, so I said that we would terminate the agency with immediate effect. We did part on good terms however.

Ayubovan – "May your life be long" is the traditional greeting in Sri Lanka, aptly named the Pearl of the Indian Ocean. For many though, a long life was constantly under threat. In the north of the island, a bitter and bloody war was raging between the forces of the Sinhalese government and Tamils who wanted an independent state. Although the main fighting was confined to the north, terrorist acts were taking place in other parts of the country, and the Colombo telephone exchange had recently been targeted. As a result, the tourist trade had vanished, and hotels, like the one I was staying, were practically empty. Up to this time in the centre and south of the island, Sinhalese, Buddhists, Hindus, and Christians seemed to have co-existed without problems.

It came as something of a surprise therefore when I met the contacts that the London company had set up for me. Chandra Kumar was a Sinhalese whilst his colleague, Srian Abeysuriya was a Tamil. Together they ran the office and got on well with each other. I felt immediately that they would be suitable for our company.

It was pointless trying to compete with the local printer whose products were adequate for many end users. Our company was now producing a range of materials using a combination of films to package powdered products.

By far the biggest market in Sri Lanka was the dried milk powder industry, and there were no fewer than four major suppliers including such household names as Nestle, Anchor, and Cow and Gate. They were importing a very thick material using aluminium foil and it was expensive. Our boffins in Bristol had developed a material using a very thin layer of metal combined with two base films, and tests had shown this to be successful in packing powder.

I had only allocated two days in Colombo thinking that Bombay and Pakistan would require much longer. This was a mistake, but Chandra managed to get appointments at all four milk powder companies. My aim was to get at least one of them to agree to test the new material. The unit cost figures were certainly very competitive and the big two, Anchor and Nestle were quick to agree to conduct trials, so I felt that I had achieved something, and if our material worked then there was a big potential here.

I wished that I had had more time here. Sri Lanka is a beautiful place with very friendly people. I was welcomed wherever I went. Some of the names of the people I met with took a bit of pronouncing. There was Mr. Wickramasingha, Mr. Wijeratne, Mr.Seneviratne, Mrs Moonesinge and Mr Vimalatheva. I now appreciate the problems that the Test Match radio commentary team get when the Sri Lankan tourists play here.

I was due to go to Bombay on the Wednesday afternoon, but Air Lanka cancelled the flight and the next one was in 48 hours time. They offered me a flight to Madras [now Chennai] with the possibility of connecting with a domestic flight to Bombay. I would have 1½ hours to connect so I thought it would be a risk worth taking.

My arrival in Madras gave me an early introduction to facets of Indian officialdom. Unfortunately the flight from Colombo was late and I was left with only one hour to connect with my onward flight. At first I thought it would not be a problem, but then I encountered the bureaucratic nightmare of Indian Customs control. I explained that I wanted to connect with the Bombay flight and that time was of the essence. That had no effect. They insisted on writing down full details of the various currencies I was carrying plus every Travellers Cheque number. Then they had to write down details of the camera I had plus the lenses and film and painstakingly, completed a massive form.

With only fifteen minutes left I thought my chances of making the flight were pretty small especially when I discovered that the domestic airport was one and a half miles away. I grabbed a taxi and after a manic dash got to the check-in desk, which had closed. However a helpful member of staff persuaded the crew to let me on so all was OK.

Taking a taxi from Bombay airport, we had not travelled but a few hundred yards when we came to a set of traffic lights. Immediately the car stopped, there was an old woman banging on the window on one side and a young boy banging on the other side. This happened every time we stopped until we reached the Taj Mahal hotel on the waterfront.

No amount of pre-reading or information from other people can prepare you for Bombay. I had heard about the poverty, dirt, and general squalor of the living conditions of countless people. I had seen the conditions of the Palestinian refugees in Jordan, so I thought I was mentally prepared. One of my brothers-in-law had served in the Merchant Navy and told me that when they approached Bombay, they met the flies two miles off shore.

What I saw was far worse than I had imagined. In other cities, I was used to wandering around the streets in my spare time, just to get a feel of the place. Here it was impossible to go anywhere on foot without being accosted all the time by beggars, not just ordinary beggars, but little girls carrying tiny babies, old ladies, men, and boys without legs or arms and boys leading blind men. The men and boys without legs sat on trolleys and propelled themselves up and down begging between the lanes of traffic.

At this time, out of an ever increasing population in Bombay of seven million, it was estimated that 1 million lived literally on the street pavements. Whole families sat against walls without any shelter. The next level, which lived on the streets, had a sheet of polythene or sacking nailed to a wall to offer some protection. This was the monsoon season with frequent heavy downpours, and the squalor and smell were unbelievable. All this right next to, reputably, one of the finest hotels in the world.

The "lucky" ones were crammed into the many shanty districts where dwellings had been erected using any kind of plastic, wood, tin or cardboard that they could get hold of. I saw open sewers with latrines on the outside of some shacks and rubbish tips crawling with people, young and old scavenging for materials which could be recycled especially anything metal or plastic.

The next strata were those "privileged" to live in high rise tenement blocks, squeezed tightly together because of the demand for space. All the time, people were flocking into Bombay from the villages in the countryside in the hope of finding a better life. Apparently, poverty in the villages was even worse than here.

I had thought Cairo to be the most crowded city in the world, but Bombay was the nearest thing to a human ant heap that I had seen. I think you will have gathered by now that my impression of Bombay was less than favourable!

Opposite the Taj Mahal hotel was "The Gateway to India" It's an impressive archway on the water's edge. It was erected in 1913 to commemorate the landing in India of King George V and Queen Mary in 1911. I would have loved to have walked across to it, as I could see from my hotel window that there were lots of street vendors and it looked a very colourful place.

I noticed that the taxis and many of the cars were of a vaguely familiar shape. I found out that the Ambassador or Amby as it is known locally was originally the Morris Oxford, which was a popular model in the UK in the 1950s. This was why it rang a bell with me. Apparently the strong framework and suspension was considered ideal to stand up to the punishment cars got on Indian roads. In 1957, Hindustan Motors bought the tooling for the model, and have been making versions ever since. They also followed the Henry Ford principle of stating that customers could have the car in any colour they liked so long as it was white!

The man running the Bombay office for the London company was an English ex-pat called Bill, and together we visited several food processing companies. All were very labour intensive with little attempt being made to modernise. Indeed the general philosophy was if it could be done by hand then why bother with a machine. "Hands" could be replaced and there was no shortage. In one company packing spices, I watched as dozens of little girls put spices into polythene bags and sealed them with a heater bar. The owner would not consider any form of automatic packing.

We visited the Cadbury factory where I thought surely modern methods would be applied but I was wrong. Even with a high unemployment rate, there still appeared to be many more people doing jobs than was necessary. In some of the well equipped office buildings, automatic lifts were installed but each lift had an attendant and as many as four or five ushers to show people in. In the offices, armies of clerks sat behind monumental piles of paper. Toilets too were manned with a man handing out paper at the urinals.

I could see little prospect of doing business in India if this was typical of the way things were done. The "red tape" involved in getting import licences led to a reluctance to consider importing our products, and I realised that it would take a considerable amount of time and effort to make any impact here. I told Bill that we would confirm the agency. He was also responsible for the Pakistan market so I hoped for better things there.

On the Saturday afternoon I took a tourist coach trip around the city. It was the only way I was going to see more of the place. The main destination was to visit the house where Mahatma Ghandi had lived. On our way we passed more of the shanty town areas and the awful shabby tenement blocks.

19 Laburnum Road, Gamdevi, was Ghandi's address when he was not touring the country preaching his philosophy of truth and non-violence. Bearing in mind Ghandi's simplistic lifestyle and appearance, it was not a surprise to find a modest building, simply furnished with a library on the ground floor containing 20,000 books. The rest of the rooms were used to depict pictures of Ghandi's life.

On the return journey, the coach took a different route, and we passed through a very affluent area of Bombay. Here among fine houses, villas, and luxury apartments lived Bombay's millionaires. What a contrast!

I asked our guide on the coach what sort of assistance was given to those desperate people on the streets. The shocking answer was "none". She explained that all these people were on a "ladder of life". If destiny placed you at the bottom then that was that. It was up to you to move up.

I left Bombay with Bill very early on Sunday morning, just as it was getting light. Already several games of cricket were taking place in the parks along the shoreline. We passed a film crew setting up a rig on an elevated stretch of road presumably for a scene in a Bollywood movie.

The contrast between Bombay and Karachi could not have been greater. Karachi's population was also around seven million, but there was no sign of the poverty and squalor that was in Bombay, no beggars or cripples hassling pedestrians and motorists. The city was just as busy with a confusion of motorised rickshaws, cyclists, motorists, horse drawn carriages, donkey carts, highly decorated lorries, and buses. People criss-crossed between all of these seemingly oblivious of any danger.

As in Bombay, Karachi had a problem with migrants leaving the surrounding countryside and trying to get a better life in the city. The problem seemed to be better handled here. Maybe it is because Pakistan is principally an Islamic State and recognises a responsibility to help the poor as part of the religion. There are tensions between Sunni and Shia communities as well as the Hindu community, which remained here after partition. Christians too form part of society.

There are many, particularly among the Shia community, who wish Pakistan to become a full Islamic state like Iran and Saudi Arabia and tolerate no other religion but Islam. For moderate Pakistanis this is a step too far, but extremism was an ongoing problem then as now. There have been assassinations, coups, and terrorist activities throughout Pakistan's brief history, and there is little sign of things getting better.

The London company had an office manned by a local and he took Bill and I to various factories. Most were far more progressive than those in Bombay and seemed to offer possibilities until I discovered that there was a 28% duty on imported packaging unless the finished product was going to be exported. Another problem was that Pakistan's credit rating was poor. Import Licences had to be obtained and whilst the bureaucracy was not as complicated as in India, several companies told me that they preferred to buy from a local printer even though the quality was inferior. Not a good start then!

On one evening we were driven to the port area. On a beach adjacent to the docks were several large ships, which had been beached and were being broken up. No health and safety regulations in operation here, just an army of men, with no protective gear, using oxy-acetylene torches to dismantle the vessels with trucks standing by to deal with the debris.

Rather than seagulls being the dominant birds, here there were the kites in large numbers, permanently wheeling and screeching in the sky from dawn to dusk.

Having covered all possible contacts in Karachi, Bill and I flew to Pakistan's second largest city, Lahore in the Punjab. I didn't see it at its best. The monsoon rain hampered getting around to our appointments and the response was more or less the same as we had got in Karachi.

The rain did relent one evening, and I went to have a look around the Lahore Red Fort, so called because of the red brickwork. It dates back to the time of the Moghul Empire and originally had twelve gates, some of which still survive. Much of the interior is faced with marble which in times past had precious stones inlaid, all gone now of course.

We were lucky in that a car journey to Sahiwal, some 150 miles south of Lahore, was completed in the dry, which gave me the opportunity to see the lush countryside sandwiched between the Ravi and Sutlej rivers. We passed areas growing wheat, cotton, tobacco, and vegetables. On the approach to Sahiwal, I saw a flock of vultures on the carcass of an animal. Nearby were huge water buffaloes wallowing in the river.

Before 1967, Sahiwal was called Montgomery after the Lieutenant Governor Sir Robert Montgomery, and we were going to see the Montgomery Biscuit Company, the oldest food manufacturing company in Pakistan we were told. The owner was an avid cricket fan, and a cricket ground was right next to the factory. Overseas touring teams used to play a fixture here. A special hostel had been built to accommodate them, and we were shown around it. I must admit that facilities looked pretty basic with bedrooms having four camp beds. Some twelve months after my visit, the England team captained by Mike Gatting stayed here. It was reported that they complained that conditions were unacceptable and that players had been kept awake by rats scurrying around the rooms. No England team ever went back and of course now no international cricket is being played in Pakistan because of security problems, which is a pity.

We flew back to Karachi where I said farewell to Bill who was going back to Bombay. I was staying in the Holiday Inn and Bill's advice was to make sure that my room was on the opposite side to the adjoining mosque. Good advice!

I delivered a full report to our MD. There was a good opportunity to be a market leader in Sri Lanka by supplying a specialised material for packing milk powder. I felt India offered little, with more problems than solutions. Pakistan just might yield some business, as some manufacturers were anxious to export and needed better quality packaging to do so.

The MD was not totally convinced about my report on India and felt that there must be opportunities somewhere here. Associate companies in Europe were clamouring for export business. We took on a clerical assistant, which was a great help to me, and also another French speaking representative. Paul had retired now so his markets needed handling at sometime.

I had two further trips to make to the Middle East before the end of the year and I agreed to tack on Sri Lanka somehow.

There was much to be done.

Chapter 20

A Most Practical Plan

The Rev. Charles Inge, a 20th century clergyman, was very impressed by the theories on self-motivation expounded by a Frenchman, Monsieur Emile Coue.

Rev. Inge wrote:

> *This very remarkable man,*
> *Commends a most practical plan.*
> *You can do what you want,*
> *If you don't think you can't,*
> *So don't think you can't, think you can.*

Emile Coue was a psychologist, who, at the end of the 19th century, developed a method of stressing optimism to gain self improvement. His motto was "Every day, in every way, I'm getting better and better." This might ring a bell with you. If you have ever seen the *Pink Panther* films with Peter Sellers as the bumbling Inspector Clouseau, you might recall his boss, the mentally deranged Chief Inspector Charles Dreyfus. He was being driven mad by Clouseau so kept repeating Coue's motto to try and preserve his sanity.

You might also recognise the words from the TV comedy series *Some Mothers Do 'Ave 'Em* when the hapless

Frank Spencer is sent on a public relations self-improvement course. His mentor, Mr Watson, tries in vain to instil this philosophy into Frank's thinking.

I could also have called this chapter "If at first you don't succeed, try, try, try again". This was written, coincidentally, by another preacher, William Edward Hickson 1803–1870.

However a travel plan was needed first, and trying to please everybody was not easy.

Having taken a break with the family, it was time to sit down and plan the remaining two trips of 1986. Normally I would have done a complete tour of the Middle East markets, but with contracts in the Gulf States tied up for the rest of the year, I decided that it was safe to leave a visit there until next year.

I started the September/October trip in Kuwait. I stayed at the Holiday Inn, which was near the airport, and also near customers on the nearby industrial area. I was now dealing direct with customers as the agency agreement with Slaiman Esh Shaya had been terminated by mutual consent as he had been "head hunted" to take over the running of the Kuwait Paper Company. Our friendship however has lasted to this day.

Whilst at the hotel, waiting in the lobby for a taxi, I saw, for the only time during my visits to the Middle East the effects of a sandstorm. Looking out of the main doors I could see that the sky was getting darker and darker and a fierce wind was blowing paper and other debris around. Then, quite suddenly it seemed, the sandstorm hit the area. You couldn't see outside. The noise of the sand hitting the building was like a severe hailstorm. Sand was being forced under the entrance doors and even started to come out of the air conditioning vents. The hotel lobby had a thin layer of sand everywhere. I suppose the storm lasted around half an hour before it either died down or moved on somewhere else. Driving to the industrial estate, the taxi had to avoid large drifts of sand, which had accumulated rather like snowdrifts.

From Kuwait to Colombo should have been straightforward because there were regular flights to meet the demand of the Sri Lankan "guest" workers in Kuwait. The flight was due to leave at 22.00 hrs but at the last moment a technical fault grounded the plane and I was told that the flight would not go before 0700hrs next morning. I was given a room at the airport hotel and realised I was the only non-Sri Lankan on the flight. I felt somewhat guilty as all the others had to spend the night in the terminal. Next morning the flight did leave at 0700hrs and for the first and only time in my travels I was upgraded to First Class. Not only was I upgraded, but I was the only passenger in that cabin and was spoiled rotten by the attendants.

Chandra Kumar had already delivered the new test materials to the three companies, which had expressed an interest, and a trial run had been arranged for me to attend at the Anchor factory. This proved to be a mixture of good and bad news. Sample packs of milk powder were put into a water pressure chamber. We were dressed in white coats and hats to protect us in case the packs exploded under pressure. Fortunately they did not, but when the packs were removed from the tank it was found that the two materials used were becoming separated. The Anchor people were sufficiently impressed with the result that they said if we could overcome this problem, orders would follow.

I was due to go to Bombay on the Sunday so on Saturday I had a rare day off. I wanted to try and see something of Sri Lanka and enquired at the Oberoi Reception desk as to what was available. All tourist activity had stopped because there were no tourists, but they offered to provide a driver to take me to Kandy and the hill country at a very reasonable price.

The driver was a very pleasant man and he said he would take me to various places of interest on the way. We set off early and our first stop was at a batik cloth dyeing place. It was all being done by hand. Batik is a process where a designer, a real craftsman or woman, traces a pattern in wax on both sides of a piece of cloth or silk with a brush or copper tool. The material is then dipped into a vat of dye and hung on a line to dry. The wax is then scraped off and the process repeated for the next colour and so on until the design is completed. The colours used were very vibrant, much in keeping with the clothes worn by the women.

Next stop was a tea plantation, which I suppose is a "must" see on any Sri Lankan tour. The manager was delighted to see a real live tourist and was keen to show me the various processes that the leaves go through. Different sections of the plantation are harvested every twenty days. The leaves are then left to dry and ferment after which they are sorted into various grades of tea. I had to confess that I wasn't a tea connoisseur. Having drunk tea of all shades and types in the Middle East and other places, I suppose my palate would not really distinguish between Earl Grey or a teabag. He made me a cup of his best quality and I did my best to be impressed. He was very dismissive of tea bags saying that only the rubbish dust gets put in them. I think of him every time I use one!

Now mid-morning, we stopped at the elephant village at Molagolo. Again this would be a natural stop for tourists, so once again I had the place to myself. This is a fascinating place where elephants are trained to work in the logging industry. From an early age, elephants are paired with an older elephant and quickly learn the trade watched over by their own mahout. Bath time was certainly something they enjoyed, and it was advisable to stand well clear! I was cajoled into riding on the back of a mature elephant. There was no seat, just a mat and a rope to hang on to. Very gingerly I climbed a platform and somehow got myself astride this giant. Then gripping the rope tightly the mahout led us around the compound. It was a strange experience and I could feel the massive power underneath me.

It was then up into the hill country, and as we climbed the mountain roads, every now and then there was a break in the trees, and with the clear air, I could see for miles. First glimpse of Kandy was the view from the top of the mountain road from Colombo. Looking down on the town I could make out the botanical gardens, the Temple of the Tooth [Buddha's] and a large lake with an island. The island was created in 1807 by the King of Kandy, Sri Wickrama Rajasinha.

We drove down into Kandy and stopped for lunch at the Queens Hotel, a historic building much loved in colonial days by the British on leave. Then after wandering through the botanical gardens full of exotic plants and flowers, I made my way to the Temple of the Tooth. The casket containing Buddha's tooth is only brought out on rare special occasions. The outside of the temple is decorated with ornate carvings with elephants very much in evidence. A huge bell with a pole striker poised for use was near its entrance. The whole site is set in beautiful gardens and is obviously a cherished place for the people of Kandy. I have seen film of the processions that take place on religious occasions with elephants wonderfully covered in rich tapestries. It must be a terrific sight.

I was very taken with Kandy and wished I could have spent more time there, but we needed to get back to Colombo. As we headed away from the town we came across a procession, which I can only assume was of some religious significance. We stopped by the side of the road to watch. I got my camera out although I was wary of using it. As the procession got nearer, I could see that it was headed by a decorated cart being drawn by two horned cows, which had garlands of flowers around their necks. Men and boys, women, and girls, many in brightly coloured clothing were clapping and singing. They waved to us, and as they obviously didn't mind my presence, I started to take some photographs. As the cart drew level, to my astonishment, I could see that it was carrying a frame from which was suspended a young man on ropes with what appeared to be meat hooks, two in his back and two in his buttocks. The entry points were covered in a white paste or powder. The man did not appear to be in any discomfort and cheerfully waved and smiled at us as he went past with those following still clapping and singing.

In better times Sri Lanka must be a fabulous place to be a tourist. The problem for them then was that much of the country was off limits because of the ongoing security situation.

My second visit to Bombay was to confirm the agency, and to follow up a couple of enquiries that Bill had obtained. Neither however looked likely to yield any business for us. My impression of Bombay did not improve especially when the car we were travelling in, was stolen whilst we were in a meeting.

Just two weeks before my visit to India, there had been an assassination attempt on the Prime Minister Rajiv Ghandi. It was thought that this had been carried out by disaffected Sikhs whom he had alienated. His relationship with the Sikhs was one of his greatest problems. It was ironic in a way that he was seen by Sri Lankans as the one man who could solve the Tamil problem, and he was responsible for sending in the Peacekeeping Force in 1987 which ended in all out war against the Tamils.

An airline pilot by profession, he had entered politics when his mother Indira Ghandi was assassinated in 1984, and he was to suffer the same fate in a bomb blast in 1991.

As a result of this attempted assassination, security was exceptionally tight at the airport, and there was a heavy military presence in the city. It was reported that all Government Ministers and Officials were now required to wear bullet proof vests weighing ten kilos which must have been incredibly uncomfortable in the hot humid weather.

Then it was Bombay to Baghdad and the news here was far from encouraging. Many foreign governments had withdrawn their lines of credit although the UK had not yet done so, but already our customers were having to reduce production and some had even shut down. I was beginning to think that our MD had the use of a crystal ball!

With the Iraq market on the verge of collapse, new markets were needed to fill the gap. Saudi Arabia was undergoing a massive industrial expansion in the three main regions of Jeddah, Riyadh and Dhahran. Dammam and Alkhobar were also neighbours to Dhahran and the three towns really merged into one.

So it was in Jeddah that I started my final trip of 1986 at the end of November. The demand for land was such that, it was being created, by pushing back the sea. This newly created space allowed developments to take place and it was a process, which continued. By the time I made my final visit to Jeddah in 1993, the Red Sea Palace Hotel was at least a mile from the new shoreline.

Whilst in the Kingdom, the inauguration of the Saudi – Bahrain causeway took place on the November 26th, and naturally dominated the news on TV and in the press. The

25 kilometre [16 miles] long causeway took five years to build and at that time, had the distinction of being the world's costliest piece of roadway. It involved the construction of a man made island out in the Gulf to serve as the frontier boundary between Saudi Arabia and Bahrain.

It was here at the frontier that the opening ceremony took place. This was carried out by King Fahd of Saudi Arabia and The Emir of Bahrain Sheikh Isa Ibn Salman Al Khalifa. The two rulers presented an odd contrast. King Fahd was a tall well built man whilst the Emir was, to put it politely, somewhat diminutive. This difference in stature seemed to cause some difficulty when it came to the official greeting between the two rulers. The traditional kiss on both cheeks was distinctly awkward to say the least, and for the official photographs, it appeared that the Emir had been given something to stand on.

Officially the causeway was due to open at the beginning of the Muslim weekend i.e. Thursday evening the November 30th, two days after I was leaving the Kingdom. I would have loved to have seen what happened because the strict rules which governed life in Saudi Arabia did not apply in Bahrain.

Hitherto, Thursday evening flights from Dhahran to Bahrain were always crammed full of Saudis and ex-pats, going there for their weekend. I think I am correct when I say that it was the shortest international flight in the world at just 10 minutes in the air.

Bahrain did not restrict the use of alcohol or frown on western dress styles. Satellite TV was available for all. The opening of the causeway would allow many more visitors to indulge themselves but Saudi authorities, fearing the worst, had let it be known that on Friday evenings, the religious police would be mounting extra checks at the frontier, and woe betide anyone returning the worse for wear.

This was not the only concern for the Saudi religious authorities. Bahrain TV Channel 55, which could easily be picked up on the east coast of Saudi Arabia, had recently started showing episodes of the American series *Dynasty*. This caused a storm of protest from Saudi Arabia. Their Press statement read: "The serial explicitly details the deviant, sexual morals of the characters, and children should be forbidden from watching it. It exposes everything bad in western society."

Bahrain responded by saying that they would suspend showing the programme during Ramadan, but then announced that they were going to start showing *Dallas*!

Just before my arrival, there had been a British Trade Week, which apparently had gone rather well even if the highlight had been a royal visit by Prince Charles and Lady Diana. At a reception at the British Embassy, a fish and chip supper was served in copies of the *Daily Mirror*, which had been flown in especially for the occasion.

New food processing factories were springing up across the Kingdom in Jeddah, Riyadh and Dhahran so I was now required to go to each area. In Riyadh construction sites were everywhere not only in the industrial areas. There were some magnificent buildings going up. One looked like a giant flying saucer. Shopping malls, hotels, offices, and apartment blocks were expanding the city, not that there was any shortage of space. Riyadh is slap bang in the middle of the desert so it keeps on growing. An effort had also been made to persuade the wandering tribes to abandon their way of life. Purpose built accommodation had been built on the edge of Riyadh but it was completely empty.

Riyadh might have been emerging as an ultra modern city, but there was still room for the camel market. I found it quite comical to see Toyota pick-up vehicles driving away with a couple of camels in the back.

It was also anticipated that Riyadh would become the administrative centre for the whole country, and that foreign embassies would be required to move from Jeddah.

Whilst there I had to deal with a rumour that one of our competitors had put about that our company was closing, and that I would be working for the competitor. Neither story was true but I had a lot of reassuring to do.

My flight from Dhahran to Colombo was full of Sri Lankan young men and women going home after completing their two year contracts. The atmosphere in the airport was almost carnival like as many friends had come to see them off, and many were carrying presents for their families as Christmas was fast approaching.

When I came to the area ten years before, it was the Philippinos who were providing the domestics and other workers. Now it was the Sri Lankans who had taken over, presumably because they were cheaper. Even in a country as rich as Saudi Arabia, they still looked after the "pennies". It was reported that the average wage of the "guest workers" was $100 a month!

Most of this income was transferred back to Sri Lanka and provided a welcome boost to their economy because in other areas the economy was suffering. The prices of tea, cotton, coconut oil, and timber had fallen sharply in the face of competition from the Far East. The tourist trade had not recovered, and a drought in the rice growing areas was raising the possibility of having to import rice.

My visits to the milk powder factories of Anchor and Nestle at last proved successful. Tests on the improved packaging had passed all the criteria necessary without any problems and first orders were placed. Officially we still needed the approval of Anchor's head office in New Zealand, and Nestle's in Switzerland, but no difficulty was anticipated here. All our company had to do now was to deliver on time, and remain competitive. At least we had a head start on the competition, but it was only a matter of time before their boffins worked out what our specification was and then the fun would start. Still we would cross that bridge when we came to it!

From Colombo I went back to India for the third time, but this time it was to Delhi. During the summer our company had been approached by an Indian company, which was considering setting up a factory for printing Cellophane and other packaging materials. They already printed tin cans and boxes, and were looking for a technology agreement.

I was asked to go and have a look at their factory and relevant facilities. I could not have picked a worse time to come to Delhi. Earlier in the week, there had been a massacre of twenty two passengers on a bus in the Punjab by Sikh extremists. Sporadic rioting followed, and a general strike hit many parts of northern India. The riots had spread to central Delhi, and a curfew had been imposed. Fortunately my hotel was in the suburbs, but getting around was going to be tricky. The Indian company sent a car for me, and took me to their factory in Gaziabad, about fifteen miles from Delhi. The roads were quiet with a lot of police on standby. What traffic there was, consisted mainly of motorbikes sometimes carrying whole families, father, mother, and up to three children. I also saw men on bicycles with huge loads strapped on the back. How they stayed upright I'll never know.

The Tin company appeared to be well run, and I reported as much to our Directors but negotiations thereafter came to nothing.

My visit to Gaziabad had been on a Friday and my flight back to the UK wasn't until Sunday, so I was hoping to see something of Delhi on the Saturday. However the disturbances in central Delhi continued so that put paid to any possible sight seeing, and hotel guests were advised to stay in the hotel.

As I looked out of the window in my room, I could see a small construction site. As I watched, a small truck arrived and dumped a load of sand about twenty yards away from a cement mixer. A man with a wheel barrow then shovelled the sand into the barrow and made several trips moving the sand nearer the mixer. Another man then put sand and cement into the mixer. Another man then started the mixer, and after due time yet another man unloaded the mixture into a wheelbarrow and took it to where it was needed. Talk about being labour intensive!

Whilst filling in time, I read copies of *India Today* and *The Times of India*, and a couple of items caught my eye.

First a headline "Broken Heart", the report read:

A 100-year-old man died recently in Ghatampur town of Kanpurdenat owing to shock, because he could not get married for the 13th time with a woman of his choice. The deceased could not marry because of obstacles put forth by his family members and other people. He is survived by 12 wives, 2 sons and 2 daughters.

The second was a joke:

Question: *Why didn't an Indian team manage to qualify for the World Cup football tournament?*

Answer: *Because each time they were given a corner, they built a shop on it!*

I did raise an eyebrow at this but in 1986 we were still cracking jokes about the Irish, Welsh, Scots and English. Not today though eh!

Victoria Peak tram and view, Hong Kong

The Gateway to India,
Bombay (Mumbai), India

Star Ferry, Kowloon, Hong Kong

Procession near Kandy,
Sri Lanka

Temple of Buddha's Tooth, Kandy, Sri Lanka

Temple, Colombo, Sri Lanka

Japanese surrender,
Sentosa Waxworks,
Singapore

The Forbidden City, Beijing

The Great Wall

Cricket on the Padang, Singapore

Guarding the Ming Tombs

Tian Fu Gong Temple, Singapore

Chapter 21

A rose-red city, half as old as Time
JOHN WILLIAM BURGON 1813–1888

The Hashemite Kingdom of Jordan always puzzled me. I got to know other Arab countries in the Middle East pretty well and what made them tick, but I never really got to grips with Jordan.

It is true to say that of all the Middle Eastern countries, Jordan enjoyed the highest regard in the crazy world of the region's politics. King Hussein had good relationships most of the time with Saddam Hussein in Iraq, President Assad in Syria and was regarded as the "senior pro" by the rulers of Saudi Arabia, Kuwait and the other Gulf States.

He also commanded respect from the UK, USA, Europe, and Russia and whilst chaos reigned all around, the country maintained a stable political position.

The high regard in which Jordan was held by practically all, did not hide the fact that, along with Syria, it was one of the poorest countries in the Middle East. It relied heavily on financial support from Saudi Arabia and Kuwait.

Jordan also was in the unenviable geographical position of being adjacent to Israel and an uneasy peace existed. Agriculture was the main industry with much of the produce finding markets in Iraq and Syria.

In the early stages of the Iraq/Iran war, Jordan became

Iraq's lifeline. The port of Aqaba was used to keep Iraq supplied with armaments and other essential supplies. Iraq took as much in the way of food as Jordan could supply, but as the war dragged on, Iraq's finances became more and more restricted, and the Jordanian economy suffered as a result, especially as the Jordanian Dinar was tied at a fixed rate to the Iraqi Dinar.

The other major headache for Jordan was the question of the Palestinian refugees. Since the Israeli occupation of Palestinian land started in 1948 followed by the 1967 conflict, Jordan had been a refuge for hundreds of thousands of Palestinians.

Many of the educated Palestinians had been absorbed into Jordan's commercial life where their skills had been put to good use. Many were allowed to take Jordanian citizenship but these were the minority. When I first visited Jordan in the late 1970s, refugee camps out in the land beyond Amman, held some two million people. I passed one of these camps on the way to a flour mill. The size of it staggered me. It was more like a tented city than a camp. Basic facilities were sparse and without the aid being given by two United Nation's agencies, UNWRA and for the children UNCHR, I'm sure their situation would have been even more miserable.

These camps, however, were the breeding grounds for recruitment to the Palestine Liberation Organisation, which caused major problems for the Jordanian authorities because of its actions against Israel. In 1970 there had been fierce fighting between the PLO and the Jordanian army.

During my various visits there was always a very visible presence by the Jordanian army, not only at Queen Alia Airport, but also on the streets of Amman. At all the major hotels in the city, armed militia were stationed at the entrances day and night.

Other wars in the region have resulted in even more refugees seeking safety in Jordan. Now, thousands of Iraqis are living there because of the ongoing internal strife, which shows no signs of ending.

Amman is an attractive city built on seven surrounding hills. There was a nice mix of old and new buildings, and the usual hustle and bustle of a Middle Eastern city. It had fine hotels run by international chains, but also many smaller, family run establishments. There was a lot for the tourist to do with many historical sites to delight those interested. Tourist trade was a vital part of the economy but blips in the country's security made the industry very fragile.

From my business point of view, up until the early 1980s, there had been little to interest us. There were two confectionery companies and one biscuit company. Their requirements were small and I had passed all enquiries to our company in Greece. The outbreak of the Iraq/Iran war gave Jordan the chance to export foodstuffs, and as a result several new companies were formed, but by the mid 1980s Iraq had restricted imports leaving companies fighting for their share of the local market.

During this period, I had become increasingly disillusioned with our agent who was also BCL's agent. They were slow to respond to telexes, and failed to spot new developments. Our companies in Greece and Holland, who were handling the business, were complaining to me about this. In addition there were now four local printers producing basic packaging. I feared that the reason for their inactivity was the same as I had found in Colombo. In other words, it was easier to sell unprinted material than our sometimes more complicated printed stuff.

The man employed by the agency to handle our business was a very pleasant Palestinian called Mohammed. He was however somewhat reticent when I put my concerns to him, and would not admit that the agency was giving us a poor service. He was an employee after all and was under instruction from the owner of the company who did not like my questioning of the efficiency of his business.

Mohammed had been granted Jordanian citizenship. His family still lived in the Israeli occupied territories so at weekends he crossed into this area to see them. The crossing was and still is at the Allenby Bridge, which spans the river Jordan. The original bridge dates back to 1918 and was built by British army engineers under the command of General Edmund Allenby. It has been replaced by a more modern construction but still retains the name.

By the time I had completed my market survey, I was even more convinced that we needed to change the agency, and on my return to Bristol I issued the termination notice. This caused a terrible fuss. The owner of the agency, which he had founded in 1922, was very, very upset. He claimed that no one had ever cancelled an agency before. He complained to our parent company, and even protested to the British Embassy. He even threatened to have me arrested on sight should I ever come to Jordan again. I did and I wasn't!

I did appoint another agent but that was a disaster for he was jailed for money laundering! After that I relied on direct contact with customers, but the damage had already been done. Our competitors and the local printers had things pretty well sewn up, and our opportunities were very limited.

My only visits to Amman afterwards were to access or depart from Iraq. Iraqi and Jordanian airlines were operating a service to and from Baghdad albeit still under the cover of darkness.

It was on one of these occasions that I had the opportunity

to go to Petra. I was on my way back from Baghdad. On this trip I had been joined by one of our company's technical experts, Mike. After ten years, much of the packaging machinery in Iraq was in great need of servicing. Spare parts were scarce, and most machine manufacturers were unwilling to send engineers into what officially was a war zone. The other problem for our customers was that many of their engineers, who had been trained to run the machines, had been drafted into the army and their inexperienced replacements had difficulties in operating the packaging machines.

Mike's visit therefore was especially welcomed by our customers. He achieved a great deal in a short time by re-setting controls and passing on advice to the new operators.

We arrived in Amman on our way back to the UK in time for Christmas. We had been fortunate in getting seats on an Iraqi Airways flight on the Thursday night but had a day to wait before getting a British Airways flight to Heathrow on the Saturday. In the Intercontinental Hotel we saw a notice from the Jordanian Tourist Board advertising a trip to Petra next day so we booked ourselves on it.

From Amman to Petra was a five hour bus ride. I say bus rather than coach. We had expected the Tourist Board to have provided a reasonably comfortable vehicle but we were wrong. The bus was a real bone shaker and after leaving at 7.30am, we arrived at a hotel on the edge of the Petra site at 12.30pm, feeling battered and bruised.

After lunch at the hotel, the guide directed us to the start of the pathway leading to the Petra site. Here was a selection of rather scrawny looking horses and we were invited to make the trip on these. Neither Mike nor I liked the look of these animals and we said we would rather walk. Five other British members of the party, two men and three women, opted for the horses.

They set off slowly ahead of us and we followed behind, but not too close!

The way into Petra is through a narrow steep sided ravine called The Siq. Being December, the temperature was very pleasant, but on entering the ravine, it suddenly got quite chilly. The vertical steep sides of the ravine, which was in places only nine feet wide, felt quite intimidating. The group on horseback was now proceeding in single file. We took our time taking in the surroundings and observing the remains of ceramic channels mounted on the sides of the ravine, which had channelled water to Petra all those centuries before. It was also clear why Petra had been easy to defend. No army could ever have penetrated through that ravine. Just a few defenders would have been able to inflict terrible losses.

We walked on, with the path getting narrower and narrower, until quite suddenly we emerged into an open space facing The Treasury, a fantastic building carved out of the red sandstone. You may have seen it in one of the Indiana Jones films. Elsewhere on the site we saw the Royal Tombs, and an amphitheatre, which could hold three thousand spectators.

The history of Petra goes back to at least 600BC, established by a tribe called the Nabataeans. It lay undiscovered for centuries until 1812 when a Swiss explorer Johann Ludwig Burckhardt discovered it. It became a "must see" place for travellers to Jordan in the 1800s and indeed ever since. One such traveller, Rev. John William Burgon was so inspired by his visit that he wrote:

Match me such marvel save in Eastern clime,
A rose-red city half as old as Time

The author Agatha Christie also visited Petra.

We were able to spend a good hour and a half wandering around the site, marvelling at the carved structures before walking back to the hotel where the bus was parked. We were very tired at the end of the day but I wouldn't have missed it for anything.

Next day we boarded the BA flight, and saw our horseback companions. They were the cabin crew and they were all walking very, very stiffly.

My summing up of Jordan – a great place to visit.

Chapter 22

Water, water everywhere nor any drop to drink

The Ancient Mariner Samuel Taylor Coleridge

So bemoaned the Ancient Mariner, and there were times on my travels when either the lack of water or too much of it made me very aware of how fortunate we are in the UK.

We complain when rain spoils our holidays or ruins a cricket match. Just occasionally, too much falls in one spot and we get disasters such as occurred in Boscastle and Cumbria. But on balance we rarely face the prospect of having no water, and water from the tap is perfectly safe to drink. It never occurs to us that it isn't.

Whilst some parts of the world get too much water, there are the others which suffer because the rains fail. The current famine conditions in the Horn of Africa are a perfect example of this.

When I first started travelling in the Middle East in 1974, my doctor, who had some experience of the area, warned me to drink plenty, but only bottled water. He said it was quite probable that I would pick up some infection caused by the preparation of food and gave me medication to cope with it. He was right!

Travelling in and over the Middle East countries quickly revealed vast areas of desert and the relatively small areas of agricultural land clinging desperately to the banks of the great rivers like the Nile, Jordan, Tigris, and Euphrates. Frequently I could see from the air, outlines of fields, which the desert had reclaimed.

When my trips started again in 1987, I was on a flight from Riyadh to Jeddah when I noticed in the desert below, a huge area of green circles. I would guess each one was around 200 metres in diameter. I then saw an article in the local paper about the project. The Saudi government had entered into a technical deal with an Irish company to grow a certain type of wheat. These green fields were being irrigated by sprays mounted on rotating arms from a central hub, which then gave the fields their circular shape. Deep bore holes provided the water source.

This was all very high tech. but compare this with the irrigation methods I had seen in Egypt. When I went to Alexandria, the road followed the Nile as it flowed north to its delta. By the fields next to the river bank, I frequently saw donkeys tied to a wooden arm being led round in a circle. This operated a simple device drawing water from the river and depositing it into irrigation channels. I suppose this method had been used for centuries.

In the Yemen mountains, terraces had been carved into the mountainsides to form small fields, which would catch the water when the rain fell.

Whereas the West gets twitchy over the supply of oil, in the Middle East it is water that has been the subject of many disputes.

Iraq is totally dependent on the Tigris and Euphrates, but the source of both rivers is not in Iraq. The Tigris rises in Turkey whilst the Euphrates also rises in Eastern Turkey and passes through Syria before reaching Iraq. Various dam projects in Turkey and Syria affected the flow of water in Iraq.

That put a severe strain on relations between these countries. If you look at a map of Iraq, you will see that these two great rivers flow north to south and that the land in between is where people live and work. The area's old name, Mesopotamia, means "Land between Two Rivers." The lifestyle of the marsh Arabs in the south of Iraq is directly affected by the river levels being maintained.

Similarly, when the Aswan Dam was constructed in the 1970s, Egyptian farmland along the Nile suffered as a consequence.

From countries lucky enough to have rivers of fresh water, I was also visiting countries that had no natural water source. Kuwait was the first in the Gulf area to build a desalination plant to produce fresh water from seawater. Similar projects were constructed in Qatar, Saudi Arabia, and the other Gulf States. This process is enormously expensive, but what choice do they have.

1987 was a troubled year. Yet another economic crisis saw stock markets crash world wide, the worst fall since 1929. Despite poor Michael Fish's assurances, a hurricane hit southern Britain causing severe damage. In Beirut, Terry Waite was taken hostage and kept captive for five years. The IRA's bombing campaign took on a greater intensity. In Bangladesh, floods destroyed 30% of this impoverished country's agricultural land.

This was the world that we lived and worked in. The sight of the green fields in the deserts of Saudi Arabia was a reminder of the technological progress that was being achieved. In my case, the slide rule had given way to the pocket calculator. I could now phone my wife Ve, every day from pretty well any part of the Middle East. This was of great benefit because the Middle East was rarely out of the media headlines, and the news was always bad so I could reassure Ve that I was fine, and of course get news from home.

The company too was embracing the new computer technology. Equipment, the size of a small room had been installed, and the hand estimating system was being replaced. Results at first did not inspire confidence in this new fangled machine, but early mistakes were rectified and a much faster turn around of enquiries meant that on occasions I could get the information I needed before I left a country.

My four trips during 1987 were fairly routine. Business in Iraq was continuing to decline and the war, now in its eighth year, showed no signs of finishing. I was determined however to maintain contact with the market and the many friends I had made there.

Sri Lanka was now providing good business through Anchor and Nestle. This had attracted the attention of the Sri Lankan Institute of Packaging, which was due to host the Asian Packaging Congress in September. They sent our company an invitation to attend and also take a display stand at their exhibition, which was to be held at the Oberoi hotel where I stayed.

I was not at all keen. My experience of exhibitions in the UK and Europe convinced me that they had never produced any worthwhile new business. Far better in my view to spend money exploring new markets at ground level. However the London company, which employed Chandra in Colombo were keen on the idea. We had a new Sales Director who also was in favour, so not for the first time I was in a minority of one, and an acceptance was duly sent.

It did occur to me that September in Sri Lanka was still in the monsoon season. This runs approximately from June to the end of September, but I thought everything would be in an air conditioned centre or hall.

I had booked my room at the Oberoi well in advance, but when the Sales Director and the London company's representative tried to book, they found that all accommodation was now taken by other delegates. Other international hotels were not far away so they booked there.

I had been in the Gulf before coming to Colombo. On arrival at the hotel, I noticed workmen in the car park erecting what I can only describe as an open sided very large tin shed. Chandra met me, bringing with him the sample packs and sales literature, which had been sent out from the UK.

To my amazement, he said that the exhibition was to be held in the tin construction that I had seen being built in the car park. Later in the day we set up our allocated stand, which was about 12ft square and fortunately, as it turned out, was raised on a wooden platform six inches deep.

Our Sales Director arrived on the morning the exhibition opened and we received a visit from the Sri Lankan Trade Minister. By the afternoon, the rains had arrived in great quantity turning the car park into a lake with rivers running between the stands. All were marooned!

The heat and humidity reduced us all to sweaty wrecks. Our stand was next to one of the milk producers and they kindly kept us supplied with cool milk drinks. As I was the only one with a room at the Oberoi, we took it in turns to go and have a shower and cool off, paddling our way to the hotel entrance.

The exhibition ran for four days and my scepticism about its value for once was correct. By the end of the four hot, wet, sweaty, and uncomfortable days, we were all in agreement that any future invitations would be declined.

On the last evening, our Sales Director, who was due to

leave next day, invited us to go out for a meal to "celebrate" the end of the exhibition. Just down the road was a famous Colombo hotel, the Galle Face Hotel. At one time, at least until the late 1970s, it had been the main hotel in Colombo. Now it was a little "tired" and needed renovation. Nevertheless, because of its historic importance, we decided to have our meal there.

Galle Face is a large grassy area, which borders the shoreline. In the days of the British Empire, it was where military parades took place as well as other ceremonial occasions. Now it is a place of relaxation where people picnic, fly kites, play games, and generally chill out.

We had our meal sitting outside. It was a fine evening and the food was very good. I was rather put off by bats flying into the ivy and other greenery, which covered the wall just above our heads. They were catching and crunching the insects, which were attracted by the outside lighting.

We asked if we could have a look around the hotel. The fittings looked to be from a very early age and compared with the modernity of the Oberoi, it was like stepping back in time to the 1920s. We came to a pair of large wooden doors, which were the entrance to the ballroom. Our guide opened them slowly and switched on a light at which point we saw a wave of cockroaches scuttle for cover. I was very glad to be staying in the Oberoi.

I made a further trip to Colombo later in the year but certainly managed to pick difficult times to enter and leave Sri Lanka. The flight from Kuwait was delayed by seven hours due, we were told, to a technical problem. That "problem" turned out to be that Sri Lanka had been paralysed by a general strike, which had been called by the outlawed JVP Communists. This was a mainly Sinhalese group, which had been banned and driven underground. They had been responsible for many terrorist actions operating in much the same way as the IRA did in the UK. A car bomb in central Colombo had killed over one hundred people, and injured many more. Such was the fear that they had instilled into the local population, that their call for a strike had been almost universally met.

At Colombo airport, the usual throng of relatives waiting to greet arrivals was totally absent. I had great difficulty in finding a taxi willing to take me into central Colombo, and when I eventually did, the one hour journey on the main road normally crowded with buses, lorries, old cars, cyclists, motorbikes, motorised rickshaws, and bullock carts all ignoring any rules of the road, took only twenty five minutes.

Several other recent bombings in Colombo had killed over two hundred people with the police, civil servants and other Government officials being the main targets. As with all of these types of bombing, many other civilians had been killed or injured in the blasts. Security was tight. Everywhere was tense, and I had difficulty in getting to see the people I wanted to see. Several in fact, came to see me at the hotel as their factories were closed.

What with the Tamil situation in the north, and these problems in the south, Sri Lanka faced an uncertain time. The Tamils were now being tackled by a "peacekeeping" force sent in from India, and reports coming out spoke of many casualties.

I was due to leave on a KLM flight to Amsterdam late at night, but the hotel received word that the JVP had launched an attack on the airport. Eventually the all clear was given, and after a taxi ride on very quiet roads, I found the airport full of soldiers. Whilst the airport had been secured, the perimeter was still being cleared and it was quite a while and well after midnight when we eventually boarded the aircraft.

The ancient mariner eventually survived all the trials and tribulations on his voyage. I was beginning to know how he felt!

Chapter 23

He must rise early that would please everybody
17TH CENTURY PROVERB

I wish I could juggle. I've always admired those street performers that I might see on occasions in Bath or acts which used to appear regularly at circuses or on the old fashioned TV variety shows. My hand/eye co-ordination is OK, and I can play bat and racquet sports without any problem, but juggling, no.

In 1988 I found myself having to juggle my time like as never before. The UK economy as usual, was in a mess, and the need to sell abroad greater than ever. However a strong Pound put our prices under threat, and profits were affected to such an extent that certain accounts were somewhat unceremoniously axed, leaving me to have to explain to some long standing customers why we could no longer accept their orders if they were unwilling to accept quite high price increases.

We were also getting complaints from some of Paul's agents and customers that since he retired, no one had been to see them.

I did an early visit to Saudi Arabia and the Gulf before trying to address this issue. The main complaint was coming from an agent whom Paul had appointed to look after the Indian Ocean territories of Reunion, Mauritius, and

Madagascar. "Wow," I hear you saying. "I wouldn't mind a problem like that."

Jacques van Mackelberg had been a good friend of Paul's. They had met when Paul was visiting Nigeria. After a messy divorce, Jacques moved to Madagascar where he set up his agency business, and Paul was only too pleased to appoint him as our company's agent. I had met him when he visited the UK and found him a very agreeable fellow, and a real enthusiast about his work. He also did some reports I understand for the BBC's World Service.

I agreed to go to the area in April, but then another complication cropped up. Our business in Colombo was going well, but Nestle said that our specification needed to be ratified by their regional technical office in Singapore. Nestle asked me to visit Singapore to get the matter sorted out quickly.

I studied the World Airways Guide trying to plan the most time effective route and finally came up with this:

Tuesday 5 April: London – Jeddah 12.30–22.20
Wednesday 6 April: Jeddah – Dhahran 18.10–20.05
Friday 8 April: Dhahran – Cairo 20.00–22.05
Saturday 9 April: Cairo – Dar Es Salaam 03.00–09.00
Saturday 9 April: Dar Es Salaam – Mauritius 10.00–14.30
Saturday 9 April: Mauritius – Reunion 17.10–17.50
Monday 11 April: Reunion – Mauritius 16.00–16.40
Friday 15 April: Mauritius – Singapore 20.40–07.25 Saturday
Monday 18 April: Singapore – Colombo 23.00–00.01 Tuesday
Saturday 23 April: Colombo – London 00.40–10.35

It was an ambitious schedule, and with hindsight, the middle section was flawed. Despite Jacques' pleas, it was impossible to fit Madagascar in as well and he said he would meet me in Reunion.

With Iraq yielding nothing, Saudi Arabia was now proving to be a worthwhile market for us. The new material, which we had supplied to the milk powder companies in Sri Lanka had been the basis of a good order obtained from a pasta manufacturer in Jeddah. He had a problem in that when the finished packs were transported around the Kingdom, many had burst by the time they were unloaded. He was getting up to a 50% rejection. On a previous visit I had successfully tested a reel of our material on his packaging machine. Then I stood on a chair and hurled the finished packs as hard as I could onto the concrete floor. Fortunately, none broke and the owner of the company was sufficiently impressed to place a good order with us. Not exactly scientific, but it worked!

My route to Reunion from Cairo meant changing planes at Dar Es Salaam and Mauritius. It was a gamble. Egyptair was never very good at timekeeping, and my connecting flight at Dar Es Salaam was with Lufthansa, which was strict on time. The flight was late arriving, and when I transferred to the Lufthansa flight, I was told that my suitcase would be transferred too. Wrong! Arriving in Reunion via Mauritius I soon discovered that my case was not on the flight. Air Mauritius promised to carry out an immediate check to find out exactly where the case was, although I was pretty certain it was still in Dar Es Salaam.

By now it was 7pm on a Saturday evening, so it was impossible to get to any shops to get a change of clothes. The hotel was way out of St. Denis, the capital, and didn't have a shop, and what was more, the laundry service had shut for the weekend. Hotel reception managed to find a toothbrush and disposable razor for me, but what I really needed to do was to get out of my sweaty clothes after that long journey.

Reunion is officially a Department of France and St. Denis is the regional capital. The island is popular with French tourists, as technically it is a domestic location.

Dodging showers on Sunday, I wandered along the coast road taking in the scenery and surroundings. It was election year in France and Reunion would be involved just as in mainland France. One of the presidential candidates was someone called Barre, and his name had been painted in white at intervals along the road surface. I hope that idea never catches on here.

Jacques arrived late afternoon, and gladly leant me a shirt and pants for which I was truly grateful. I also received a message from Lufthansa. My case had been located in Dar Es Salaam and would be available for collection in Mauritius on Monday.

There wasn't time to see much of the rest of this small island. Jacques had hired a car for 24 hours and we went to see two small snack food companies. I had quite a shock when we met the first owner. He was Chinese, and Jacques told me that many businesses here had Chinese owners. I never did find out what had brought them here. He had a very nice house on a hillside overlooking St. Denis. His small factory was located behind the house. We spent a very pleasant hour sitting on his balcony, sipping cold drinks and discussing future designs for his packaging.

The impression I got on this short visit was that all the habitation and industry was situated around the coastline, because the centre of the island was dominated by two active volcanoes, although they posed no threat. The main road ran around the coast hugging the shore, and in places, tunnels had been carved through rocky outcrops.

Our flight to Mauritius on Monday afternoon was in complete contrast to the one I had come in to Reunion. That was on a 747 whereas the flight to Mauritius was to be on a small Twin Otter aircraft. Having boarded and feeling somewhat cramped, I was puzzled by the appearance of a stewardess for there was nowhere for her to go. Just as the door closed, she pushed in a container of carton drinks and some packs of biscuits and told us to share them round. Then she left us!

I could quite see why Mauritius was my old boss Paul's favourite place to visit. It certainly is a beautiful island, and unlike some other tropical destinations, I could see no signs of poverty amongst the local inhabitants.

Jacques hired a car at the airport, and we drove to Curepipe, a small town in the centre of the island. All the hotels in Port Louis, the capital, were full, so we had to settle for rooms in the grandly named Continental Hotel. I'm sure it had seen better days at one time, and certainly did not appear in any holiday brochures. My room was relatively clean, but the air conditioning was very noisy when, that is, it was working. I had now been reunited with my suitcase. A change of clothing was now no problem, and a laundry service was available.

Also available was a "massage" service offered by a "lady" named Jasmin who patrolled the corridors. I declined the offer politely. After all it wouldn't have looked too good on my expense claim form would it?

It was a spectacular ride into Port Louis. Curepipe was quite high up, and with a high mountain range in the distance, the road took us past fields where sugar cane was grown. Sugar cane fields covered almost half the island, and exports to Europe, USA, and Canada were vital to the island's economy. Sugar, in the past, had been the top foreign exchange earner for Mauritius, but now it had been overtaken by earnings from a growing textile industry. It had earned a reputation for high quality work and had contracts from many of the top brands in Europe. Tourism at this time was a relatively new thing, and large luxurious complexes were being built around the island's coastline, so on three fronts, the outlook for Mauritius' economy was looking good.

Jacques was obviously well respected by our clients and we didn't appear to have competition for our business with the local confectionery and biscuit companies. We were also supplying material to an Anchor milk powder factory following our success in Sri Lanka. It made a very pleasant change working here and I promised Jacques that I would come back in twelve months, and also include Madagascar on the schedule.

Regrettably, there was no time to relax, and on the Friday I took an overnight flight to Singapore arriving at Changi airport at 7.25am. Immigration procedures were swift, but Customs' checks were very thorough. They are constantly on the lookout for drugs, and anyone caught can expect harsh penalties.

It was around 9o'clock when I came through Arrivals and took a taxi. As we neared the city centre, the taxi pulled into a lay by and switched the engine off. The driver told me that in order to reduce rush hour congestion, taxis were banned from the city centre between 9 and 10am. It was half an hour before he was able to take me to the hotel.

After the Continental Hotel in Curepipe, the Marina Mandarin hotel was pure paradise. Showered, shaved and after a couple of hours rest, I went walkabouts. The hotel was situated near the sea front, and the old colonial administration buildings were close by. These included the Supreme Court, City Hall, the Memorial Hall, and the Victoria Theatre, all steeped in the history of the British Empire. In front of these was a large grassy area known as the Padang. This is the home of the Singapore Cricket Club and being a Saturday, a match was taking place. It looked as if the old colonial days had never gone away. I did notice how spotlessly clean everywhere was. Litter is very much frowned upon, and chewing gum is banned.

There might have been some links with the past, but Singapore was definitely moving forward with an energetic, almost aggressive, approach to its economy. It had one of the world's busiest ports. Commodities such as tin, rubber, coconut oil, rice, timber, jute, spices, and coffee are all exported from here. I also faced competition from a packaging company here, which was selling into Sri Lanka and the Gulf States. We could not compete with their prices. Large oil refineries operated on outlying islands and Singapore is one of the world's key financial centres.

I received a message from Nestle's technical office to say that they would see me at 9.30am on the Monday. So Sunday was my day off. I found that the tourist industry operated a coach system, which travelled around the major hotels taking guests to see the sights, so I signed up for a tour.

The coach duly arrived on time. First stop was the Tian Fu Gong Temple. Because of the narrowness of the alleys leading to the Temple, the coach parked a couple of blocks away. Our guide led us through a less salubrious part of Singapore, one which I would imagine dates back to pre-war times. These blocks were run down flats and have probably been replaced by now with more modern dwellings.

Tucked behind was the Temple, dwarfed by skyscrapers in the background. The place was packed, not only with sightseers but also worshippers who didn't seem to mind us. Altars were decorated beautifully with vivid red and gold drapes, which were embroidered with oriental designs, dragons being very much in evidence. At one side, a priest was standing being handed prayers or messages that worshippers had written. Next to him was a small open stove, and he was putting the papers on to the fire. The ashes and smoke were then drawn up into a chimney taking the messages to their dear departed loved ones now in heaven. I suppose we all think of heaven as somewhere "up there" and it seemed a nice idea to me.

Next stop was the world famous Raffles Hotel named after Sir Stamford Raffles, and opened in 1886. After a coffee [expensive] we were shown around the ground floor. It had been restored to its pre-war opulence when it had been a "Mecca" for princes, lords, maharajahs, film stars, and other celebrities of that era. We were shown the "Writer's Bar" inspired by the great writers who had frequented it, such as Rudyard Kipling, Joseph Conrad and Somerset Maughan. No doubt they sampled many Singapore Slings! Photographs of the rich and famous adorned the walls, and despite some modernisation, the place still retained that old colonial feeling.

We were due to take a cable car ride to Sentosa Island, but it was out of operation, so the coach took us instead. This was disappointing as I could see that the cable car would have offered superb views of Singapore.

The main attraction on the island was a museum of wax works depicting life in the early part of the 20th century, then the Japanese occupation, and finally a remarkable reenactment of the surrender of the Japanese to Lord Louis Mountbatten. The figures were extremely lifelike, and I almost expected them to move, they were that good.

The actual surrender ceremony took place at the City Hall Municipal Buildings on the September 12th 1945. Lord Mountbatten together with British, American, Dutch, Australian, Indian, and French military personnel accepted the surrender from General Seishiro Itagaki and five other Japanese commanders. General Itagaki also handed over his two ancient swords, an act of great significance. The ceremony ended with the raising of the Union Jack, one, which had been kept hidden in Changi prison during the occupation.

It was now lunchtime, and we headed for the Botanical Gardens and its café. The gardens were certainly beautiful, but we were told to go and see the collection of orchids. I did, but not knowing anything about them, their significance was rather lost on me.

It was at this point that a tropical storm hit Singapore. We were some two hundred yards from the coach park, and we all got drenched in getting back to the coach. The driver, to his credit, decided that a trip to the zoo was not on in these conditions with us all steaming gently. He took us to a pewter factory instead, run entirely by physically handicapped people. The standard of their work was fantastic. I bought a couple of tiny pieces as I wanted to support their work, and it was nice to know that in an ultra modern state like Singapore, these good people were not being sidelined.

On Monday morning, I duly went to the Nestle office in an industrial area. There I submitted our technical specification and received a signed acceptance to be handed to Nestle in Colombo plus a copy for us. I also obtained a confidentiality agreement regarding our specification. It might have bought us some time although I knew that if our competitor's boffins were any good, it was only a matter of time before they had worked out what our material consisted of.

Then it was back to Colombo. The general situation in the country was getting worse. It was all out war in the north with the Tamils whilst the Communist JVP activists in the south were targeting individual government members, several of whom had been assassinated. Such was the tension and worries over security that many major airlines had pulled out. Only British Airways and KLM remained and they were due to pull out shortly.

Although we were still getting orders, the outlook did not seem promising. I really felt sorry for the people of this beautiful country. They deserved better than this.

As for juggling, now I come to think of it, I can't even dance!

Chapter 24

East is East, and West is West
And never the twain shall meet
Till earth and sky stand presently
At God's great judgement seat

So declared Rudyard Kipling who, about 100 years ago, had returned from his time in India and the Far East including Singapore. What would he have made of the world today and China's position in it? Without doubt there would be products in his house marked "Made in China".

I was lucky enough in 1989 to make two visits to China although the intervening period was marred by tragic events.

In preparing for a visit to the Indian Ocean Territories in April, I was asked by our UK sales director to investigate a problem, which had arisen with one of the major UK accounts. Their client was the largest importer of peanuts in the UK. For a long time, they had suffered as a result of consignments from China arriving in the UK in poor condition.

Technology in the packaging world never stands still. I spend more time in supermarkets looking at the new ways in which food products are being packaged, than I do in actual shopping! By 1989, new materials had come into the packaging world. Cellophane was being replaced by materials derived from the petro-chemical industry, such as polypropylene, nylon, and polyester. Combinations of these materials were offering a wide range of options for packing all sorts of products including liquids.

The UK customer had bought a quantity of large laminated pouches capable of holding up to twenty five kilos of peanuts. A machine had been installed in the peanut processing factory in Dong Guan, China, which would vacuum pack the peanuts, then seal the pouch so that the contents would arrive in the UK in perfect condition. That was the theory anyway but consignments were still arriving in a poor state. Our product was being blamed and we were facing claims for compensation.

I was asked to meet their company representative in Hong Kong, and he would arrange for me to go to Dong Guan to see for myself what was happening. A visa would be obtained for me on arrival.

Fitting Hong Kong into my flight schedule proved rather tricky and in the end I had to go to Johannesburg from Mauritius to connect with a South African flight direct to Hong Kong. This wasn't straightforward, as for some peculiar reason, no transit facilities were available for the transfer to the Hong Kong flight. I was given a hard time by a stroppy immigration official wanting to know why I had entered South Africa without a visa or entry permit. Even when I showed him the ticket for my onward journey a couple of hours later, he wasn't very impressed. Eventually he relented, and I made my way quickly to the departure lounge.

After a long overnight flight, we approached Kai Tak airport. I had heard stories about this airport, and it was of little comfort to know that it was classed as the sixth most dangerous in the world. The Captain warned passengers not to be alarmed at what they were about to see. The 747 then banked steeply and flew between skyscrapers on its final approach. It was unnerving to see people looking out of their apartment windows. They seemed close enough to shake hands with. Crosswinds were the pilot's biggest problem especially as the landing strip extended out into Victoria Harbour. It seemed ages before the aircraft came to a stop just before the end of the runway.

Kai Tak was closed in 1998 and replaced by a new airport at Chep Lap Tok about twenty miles to the west and with less challenges for incoming aircraft. If you would like to see Kai Tak for yourself, I recommend you watch the videos on YouTube.

Initially I found Hong Kong quite overwhelming. The noise, speeding traffic, and skyscrapers crammed together all felt intimidating. Taxis, buses, and trams competed for space with cars, motor bikes, cyclists and pedestrians. There wasn't any space that wasn't being used.

In the afternoon I made my way by taxi to the address of the contact I'd been given. The contact turned out to be a she not a he. She was a well built Chinese lady whose name, regretfully, I've forgotten. She said that an appointment had been made at the factory in Dong Guan next day, and that she would meet me in the morning at the appropriate Pier Head, which would be clearly sign posted. She said I would get my visa at the Chinese border.

I was really looking forward to the ferry trip. Hong Kong harbour was a spectacular mix of old and new vessels. The old junks and barges were particularly fascinating, and I anticipated a good time with my camera. The ferry left at 9am, and the Pier was well sign posted as promised. Unfortunately the ferry was a hovercraft so all passengers were inside, and the spray which was thrown up prevented any decent views outside. The trip took about an hour and we disembarked at the Chinese border on the Pearl River.

I was the only foreigner, and a young Chinese soldier in a small breeze block building, regarded me somewhat suspiciously, but after a short conversation with my companion, stamped a twenty four hour visa in my passport.

My guide then negotiated with a taxi driver to take us to Dong Guan, a journey of about forty miles. It was now 10.30am. The paved road ran out after a couple of miles, and we were being driven, at a slow pace, along a dirt road which was on a high embankment overlooking rice paddy fields on either side. Our slow pace was caused by other cars, lorries, bullock carts, motor bikes, cyclists, and tractors. This traffic was coming and going in both directions so overtaking was impossible.

It was therefore 12.30pm before we reached Dong Guan City, and my companion said there was no point going to the factory as it would be closed for lunch. So, with the driver we found a restaurant. Chicken and rice seemed to be the only dish of the day. I am hopeless with chopsticks but fortunately other utensils were supplied!

I was impressed with the layout of the roads in Dong Guan. Katie Melua has a song *Nine Million Bicycles In Beijing*. Dong Guan had a lot too, and they had a dedicated road lane, which was being well used.

We arrived at the factory at 2.30pm but the manager was nowhere to be seen. By the time he turned up, it was nearly 3pm. We had one eye on the clock because the last ferry back to Hong Kong left at 6pm and I only had a 24hour visa.

The packing process was started and I examined the finished product. Even to my non technical eye, I could see straight away that the final seal after the vacuum process, was not even and would easily give way under pressure. The slightest bump would have caused the seal to give way and release the vacuum. They tried increasing the temperature but still could not maintain an even pressure along the length of the seal. It was clearly a machine problem not a material one. Rather grudgingly, the manager agreed, and said they would refer the matter to the machine manufacturer. There was no name on the machine, and I suspected that it was Chinese made.

By now it was after 4pm leaving us only two hours to get back to the ferry. Our journey was just as chaotic as the inward one, and it soon became obvious that we were not going to get to the ferry terminal by 6pm.

The driver was persuaded to drive a further thirty miles east towards the land border between China and Hong Kong, where we could catch a train. The station was still some miles away from the border, and it was dark by the time we got there. Eventually a train came, and as we started to get near to the border, I could see, through the carriage window that the whole area was lit up by floodlights revealing massive construction projects. This was the beginning of China's economic revolution. My companion told me that factories in Hong Kong were closing, and work transferred to this area because of cheaper labour than Hong Kong.

Passport checks at the stations on either side of the border were very thorough, and I could not help noticing the very high barbed wire fencing on the Chinese side. It was ironic in a way because within a couple of months, the UK had agreed to hand over control of Hong Kong to China in 1997.

I thought that this would be my only chance to see this part of the world but another opportunity presented itself almost immediately. Mrs Thatcher's government was very keen to promote good commercial relations with this growing economy.

China was now led by Chairman Deng Xiaoping who had taken over in 1978, two years after the death of Chairman Mao. He was considered a reformer, and gradually opened up China to foreign investment. He is also credited with having the vision of China's economic expansion. This required much needed technical assistance, and the UK was one of several European countries approached to provide it.

Major British companies were encouraged to take part in an industrial exhibition, which was to take place in Beijing in November 1989.

Our parent company Courtaulds agreed to take part, and issued instructions to British Cellophane and ourselves to represent them. The necessary registration forms were completed and the fees paid.

However, the reform of the political system in China was proving to be a slow process. Demonstrations demanding change broke out in Beijing in April, and in other large cities. Things came to a head when in June, the army was sent in to clear Tiananmen Square in Beijing, which had been occupied by students and other protesters. It was estimated that 500,000 people occupied the square. The pictures of the events that followed shocked the world. The photograph of the man in a white shirt standing in front of a line of tanks stopping their progress, is one of the most iconic of the 20th century. The man is then seen to climb on the tank to speak to its driver before getting down and standing once again in front to block its path. He is then seen to be pulled into the watching crowd. His identity is not known but he is believed to have been killed along with many others that day, June the 4th. Figures of those killed in the square and surrounding streets vary from hundreds to thousands.

Universal international condemnation followed, and I naturally assumed that the exhibition in November would be cancelled. These events, and the world's reaction to the way in which China had dealt with them, clearly shook the Chinese government. Intense diplomatic activity followed as they went to great lengths to persuade the world that things would change for the better. It was an assurance that Mrs. Thatcher accepted, and British companies were urged to attend the fair. This plea met with a mixed response, but Courtaulds took the decision to go as planned.

I went first of all for a week in Saudi Arabia, and then took a flight from Riyadh to Beijing via Bangkok.

It was 10pm when we landed. The connecting flight from Bangkok had been delayed by two hours. I had been told that I would be met but, having cleared immigration and customs, found nobody waiting. I hung around for a while but it was now after 11pm. The airport was quiet and all the taxis had gone. It was also bitterly cold. The temperature in Riyadh had been a pleasant 20°c and here it felt like minus 20°c. Two young Chinese men came across and asked if I would like a lift into Beijing, which was twenty miles away.

Normally I would have refused, but in the circumstances, and much against my better judgement, I accepted their offer. I need not have worried. In their old car they drove steadily into central Beijing. They said that they dared not drop me outside my hotel in case the police stopped them, so I got out about fifty yards away. They didn't ask for payment but I had a few US dollars with me and they accepted them gladly. Whatever people in the world feel about the USA, I always found that the dollar was universally welcomed!

Next morning, I linked up with two colleagues from

British Cellophane, and we headed for the Exhibition Hall. On the way I stopped off for a quick visit to "The People's Store" to buy a duck down filled anorak. This now comes in handy on cold winter days watching Bristol Rovers!

The Exhibition centre was very near to Tiananmen Square. Originally over seven hundred firms had signed up to exhibit in this huge hall, but only sixty turned up because of the summer's events. The Chinese authorities made a great fuss of us, and we were invited to visit the No. 1 Confectionery Factory, which didn't have quite the same ring about it as Cadbury's!

We were taken by car to an enormous factory where dozens of little girls were wrapping sweets by hand. In another section we saw brand new packaging machinery imported from England, still wrapped in polythene. We asked why it wasn't being used and were told it was for the future. The factory wanted to export sweets but the standard of packaging was so poor that they couldn't find a market. I showed them our design folders for comparison, and had the feeling that it wouldn't take them long to catch up.

Near to our stand at the centre, was a Chinese company demonstrating a printing machine, which was a smaller version of a machine we had in Bristol. It was producing a high quality end result so the No 1 Confectionery Factory would have a good local source. When I enquired how much it cost, they said £40,000. Our machine had cost over £1million.

Our time on the stand was pretty boring as it was at most exhibitions. We were displaying dummy packs, which had been used at the Interpack Fair at Dusseldorf in the summer. There was no product inside and they stood on shelves protected by retaining ropes. One afternoon, a man reached across and took one. He then bolted for the exit pursued by two security guards who grabbed him and frog marched him off. Poor chap, we never found out what happened to him, but I bet it wasn't just a caution.

We had an interpreter on the stand, Cheng Zhu, a tiny young lady who was good fun. She worked for the Danone company office in Beijing. She lived with her husband and her parents in one of the many high rise apartment blocks. She insisted that we say "Good Morning" in Chinese every morning. I don't know how you spell it but it sounded like "knee how"!

The exhibition carried on over the weekend. On Saturday it was an "open day" for students and hundreds descended on the Exhibition. We were kept busy answering questions. Nearly all had good English and many pleaded with us to find them jobs in the UK or USA. No mention was made by anyone of the terrible events of a few months back. There were plenty of security people around so it would have been most unwise of the students to raise the subject for fear of being overheard.

We took it in turns to have some time off, so on Sunday, I booked myself on a day trip to see the Great Wall and the Ming Tombs. A mini bus picked up myself and several others including the Peruvian Charge D'Affaires and his family who were good company.

The Ming Tombs were thirty five miles from Beijing and it took us a good hour to reach them over bumpy somewhat empty roads. The thirteen tombs are scattered over an area of forty square kilometres but only one, the Ding Ling, the tomb of the 13th Ming Emperor, had been excavated so far. The way leading to the tomb entrance was guarded by stone figures of lions, camels, elephants and fierce looking warriors. We were led to the underground chamber twenty seven metres below the surface. It was even colder than the outside temperature. Here we were shown various artefacts, which had been discovered.

The Chinese seem to have a passion for feeding visitors because we were then taken to the Ding Ling Restaurant where a meal of rice, meat, vegetables and a few other ingredients which I did not recognise, had been laid on.

Then it was off to the Great Wall another twenty miles away. Here there were crowds of locals as well as other foreign tourists. At the foot of the steps leading up to this section of the wall, was a sign which read, "Matters to be noted. Don't carve or write anything on the Great Wall. Don't spit or litter. No smoking in the area." I did wonder why the sign was only in English and Chinese. There were plenty of guards to make sure everyone behaved.

The section of the Wall that we had come to was called the Badaling Ridge. It is eight hundred metres above sea level and was an important fort. On the top it is wide enough for ten people to walk side by side and in olden times was wide enough for a chariot to travel along. It was bitterly cold but the winter sunshine showed the wall off at its best. As I walked along I was stopped several times and asked to take a photograph of a couple or group, and of course I had a good time with my own camera.

The next day, I used my lunch break to walk to nearby Tiananmen Square, now strangely quiet. I walked across to the Forbidden City, paid a small entrance fee, and went in. Until 1911 this was the Imperial Palace, and had been the home of Chinese Emperors for five hundred years. The site is full of ornate palaces, pavilions, gardens, theatres, gatehouses, and watchtowers. I didn't have a lot of time but squeezed in as much as I could in an hour. If you ever get the chance to see the film *The Last Emperor* you will see much of the city as it was used as the film set. The halls had exhibitions of ceramics, paintings, and gold objet's d'art. In one room I saw an amazing collection of ornate clocks, and in another, a glass case containing a pile of nail clippings from one of the Emperors.

Beijing had a new underground railway system, and one of my colleagues wanted to try it out. One evening on the way back to the hotel he persuaded a rather bemused taxi driver to drop us off at one station, and then pick us up three stops up the line. He looked at us as though we were mad, and come to think of it – well! He duly obliged, and I bet he had a good tale to tell to the other cab drivers about the crazy English.

I know I was very fortunate to see what I did in China. Things were changing, and I came home via Hong Kong. I visited our company's oldest client. They had bought from us for over thirty years and were in the process of transferring production across the border into China. They too quoted the reason as labour costs, and weren't prepared to wait until 1997 when Hong Kong would become part of China again. I also made enquiries about the peanut factory in Dong Guan and was told that the factory was now closed because the peanut harvest in northern China had failed.

I had a free afternoon on my last day in Hong Kong and took the ferry to Kowloon. The fare was equivalent to 5p. I then went up on the rack railway to the top of Victoria Peak where there were magnificent views of the whole area.

I had really enjoyed the experience of the last week, but I knew that from a business point of view there would be no real opportunity for us here at present.

Chapter 25

And take a bond of fate

MACBETH WILLIAM SHAKESPEARE

Every year, at the beginning of January, the export team would be asked to submit their sales forecast for the financial year ahead, i.e. April – March.

We were supposed to take the task seriously, and I suppose in one way we did. My old boss Paul, decided back in the 1970s that such a demanding job required a quiet and non distracting atmosphere, so we usually relocated to a north Somerset pub for most of the day and tried to put together some figures that would satisfy the powers that be. Plenty of coffee and a good pub lunch were of course obligatory.

The trouble we very quickly found out with any forecast of this nature, was that foreign governments, dictators, civil wars, natural disasters, changes in fiscal policy, plus fluctuations in the value of world currencies, all conspired to render our forecasts pretty meaningless.

Despite these "inconveniences", we usually managed to achieve and even surpass the total that we had predicted. One or other of the markets we dealt with would produce surprise results, or a totally new market would suddenly open up to us.

So in January 1990, although Paul had long since retired, we once again sat down to work out a forecast for 1990/1. I was anticipating great things for Iraq. The war had ended in July 1988. In visits to Iraq during 1989 I had found great optimism about the future. With the strength of its oil revenue, it was anticipated that the country's financial position would recover quickly. So on an early visit to Iraq in February 1990 I had hoped to find that our customers had obtained their import licences, which were usually issued in January. What I found was that their mood of optimism had vanished and been replaced by frustration. Companies had not been given any indication of when licences would be granted. Of even greater concern to our company was the fact that the Iraq central bank had failed to transfer outstanding payments.

I went back on a short visit a couple of months later, but nothing had changed. Everyone found out why when on August 2nd Saddam Hussein ordered his army into Kuwait.

I knew that Slaiman and his family were safe because they had relocated to the USA in the 1980s when it seemed possible that Kuwait would be drawn into the Iraq/Iran war. Bernhard [the Arsenal fan] escaped by driving along with countless others across the desert into Saudi Arabia.

Suddenly my Middle Eastern market was looking decidedly bare. However during the summer, I was contacted by an engineer based in Blackpool. He told me that he was about to go to Khartoum in the Sudan to refurbish confectionery and packaging machines, which had lain idle for over twenty years.

As Iraq now became a pariah state, so that status was lifted from the Sudan as United Nation's sanctions were lifted. The UN was satisfied that after twenty years of civil strife and poor government, the country was now stable enough for normal relations to be resumed. I knew that Paul had done good business there in the 1960s but visas were difficult to get. However we received an enquiry via the London office of a Sudanese company which had a sugar processing factory. I had a meeting with them and told them of my intention to visit Sudan. They said that they would arrange for me to get a visa on arrival in Khartoum, so I made plans to go in September.

Egypt was still available to me and we had two good ongoing contracts there, so Cairo was my first stop before going to Khartoum.

Work had already started on a new Khartoum airport. The current one was very dilapidated, and on reaching the immigration desk I handed over my letter of introduction, which the Sudanese London office had given me. I was shown into stiflingly hot room and sat there with several other people for almost an hour before my passport was returned with the appropriate visa stamped in it. The airport was quite central and I took a taxi to the only hotel of note The Hilton.

Khartoum, Khartoum North, and Omdurman are three cities merged together around the junction of the Blue and White Nile. From this point the Nile flows north all the way through Egypt to the Mediterranean. Apart from the hotel, the whole area was terribly run down. Old colonial style buildings in wide boulevards were evidence of the old French and British colonial rule. They were now shabby and in an awful state. I saw open sewers and broken water mains spewing out this valuable commodity. The streets were littered with piles of rubbish. The years of poor government had taken their toll.

I went to the confectionery factory where the engineer from Blackpool was working. He had taken on a very difficult job taking the machinery apart piece by piece to clean and reassemble. In one feed pipe he had found the skeleton of a rodent, and immediately behind it the remains of a small snake which had chased it there.

Other sweet companies were nearing the stage when they could start production, and I also found a biscuit company. So business prospects were good, as they were also with the sugar factory.

The Kenana Sugar Factory had been opened in 1980 and was the brainchild of the late "Tiny" Rowland, whose Lonrho Company had extensive operations in Africa. Older readers may recall the many battles he had with Mohammed Al Fayad over Harrods in London. As part of an agreement with the Sudanese government, a plantation and processing factory were established at Kenana, which is near Rabak on the eastern bank of the White Nile, some 156 miles south of Khartoum. The sugar, which was produced over the first few years, was of low grade quality intended for local use. However by the time that I was introduced to the company via their London office, the quality, especially the whiteness of the sugar, matched that of the major refiners. They were now looking to export sugar and were aiming to sell to Saudi Arabia and the Gulf States. Paper packaging such as we have in the UK, would not have been any good because of the humidity, so moisture proof material was required.

Two German packaging machines had been imported from a company I knew well, and they had successfully tested some of our material before despatching the machines so when it came to negotiating the first order we were well placed. There was one slight hitch in that before we got the OK to produce a bulk order, Kenana wanted to test material printed with their design on site and I was requested to attend. A small amount was printed and sent out by airfreight.

I had arrived in Khartoum on Friday. The next two days were spent visiting the companies still getting their factories ready for production. I had set aside Monday and Tuesday for the trip to Kenana before returning to the UK on Wednesday. Their London office told me that the Khartoum office would arrange transport and also arrange the necessary paperwork to get me through the military checkpoints en route. Civil war in the south of the country was threatening to spread northwards into the Kenana region which was still under military control to maintain a buffer against possible rebel attack.

By "transport", I had hoped that this would be by the light aircraft, which appeared in the company brochure, but no such luck. My trip was to be on the company bus, which left every day taking workers to and collecting them from the factory. Start time was 5am. The bus reminded me of one of those vehicles, which appeared on our roads just after the war. I doubt very much that it would have passed an MOT test.

At least the early start meant that for two or three hours, the temperature would be reasonable but by 8.30am it was getting uncomfortable. The bus did have blinds but they did little to make any difference. A stop was made at a wayside shack in the middle of the desert. Outside was a big tank of water with large blocks of ice floating in it. Where on earth the ice had come from I don't know. In the tank were bottles of Coca Cola so we all bought one. Round the back were basic crude "facilities" and the less said about them the better! Back on the bus we trundled on, passing the occasional mud hut village. As we went further south, the military checkpoints got more frequent. The special document, which the Khartoum office had given me was all in Arabic, but I guessed it was their permission to visit their factory and it passed scrutiny.

Around 10 o'clock we started passing fields of sugar

cane, which seemed to stretch as far as the eye could see, and then we arrived at the factory site. This was a huge mill in the midst of other buildings and a residential compound. Nearby was a village of mud and straw houses where the field workers lived. The fields of sugar cane were at various stages of growth, and were irrigated by channels of water pumped from the nearby Nile. I contrasted the sophistication of this operation with a scene I had witnessed from my room at the Hilton. Out of a window I could see a small area being cultivated by one man with a tool like a potato hoe. His water supply was also the river but he had to fetch it in a bucket, and I watched him make repeated trips to water his crop.

I was given a tour of the site by the manager, and saw all the various processes that the cane went through before becoming the finished refined sugar. The tests on our material took quite a time. The machine operator was not experienced but eventually got all the right settings in place, and the finished printed packs looked very smart. I took several packs to hand in to the Khartoum office next day hoping that they would give the OK to proceed with the bulk order. I had a meal with the manager that evening in his compound accommodation, which was fine and he, kindly let me use his spare room for the night.

Next morning, the bus from Khartoum arrived at 10am and along with workers, I boarded for the return trip. We hadn't travelled very far when the bus had a puncture. We all had to get out into the hot sun whilst the driver jacked up the bus and put on the spare wheel. All this took over an hour, but eventually we were under way again. We got about two thirds of the way back and beyond the refreshment shack when the bus had another puncture. No spare wheel this time and much head scratching! We still had some fifty miles to go and with no other help available, the situation required delicate handling. Fortunately, if that is the right word, the puncture was in the rear wheel on the near side so very gingerly he drove at about fifteen miles an hour with one front and one rear wheel on the soft desert sand. We made it back to the office in Khartoum just as they were closing at 5pm. I handed in the packs. They were pleased with the results, and gave permission to print the order.

I was to visit Khartoum a further three times over the next two years. Although industries were now up and running and we were getting useful business, there was little sign of any improvement in the infrastructure with the exception of the airport, which by the time of my last visit, had been completely rebuilt.

Earlier in the year, I had visited more of Paul's old markets to see if we could obtain more orders. First stop was Madagascar, which pleased Jacques no end. On the flight path to this huge island, long before land was in sight, I could see that the colour of the sea had turned a ruddy brown. As we flew in over the coast, I could see that on the mountains that sloped down to the sea, all the trees had been felled so that when the tropical rainstorms occurred soil was being washed into the sea.

Arriving at Antananarivo airport, our exit from the aircraft was followed by an undignified scramble up an outside metal stairway to get to the immigration desk. There was no orderly queue, just a couple of hundred people trying to be first. I did have the last laugh though because as I went to the baggage claim area, I saw my case coming up the carousel first, the only time it ever happened on my travels.

I was only here for a day and a half as we only had two customers. I was immediately struck by the vivid colours, first the bright red tiles on the roofs of houses and second, by the bright green of the vegetation. The small fields that we passed on the way to see a client looked well tended, and all had white egrets feeding on them.

I did come back again for a very short visit the next year and met Jacques' charming wife who was a local lady. I stayed this time at their house, and late at night heard some strange chanting. Jacques said that it was coming from a group meeting nearby who followed voodoo, which apparently was common in Madagascar. I would love to have spent more time here but we had to move on to Reunion and Mauritius.

From Mauritius I went to Nairobi, again to see if any of Paul's old contacts could provide more business. Our Agent, Amin told me that our one customer, a confectionery company, was mainly using unprinted material. We did however look at another possibility. Immediately alongside Nairobi airport, a large area of cultivation was producing soft fruits, tomatoes and a lot of other vegetables. These were for export and were being despatched on a daily basis by air to markets all around Europe. I knew that Marks & Spencers had been supplied from here. At this time, produce was being sent in cartons but it seemed only a matter of time before some of the big names wanted packaged goods, which could be on the shelves within 24 hours. Amin was going to keep an eye on this industry.

At another meeting in central Nairobi, Amin parked his car outside the offices. There were no parking restrictions but he paid a small group of young men to guard the car. This apparently was common practice in Nairobi!

Again I was only here for two days. I had a meal with Amin and his family and he offered to show me something of the nearby countryside. There were still a few hours of daylight left. His two children came along for the ride, and we headed north, first along a paved road and then on a wide dirt road when the paved one ran out on the outskirts of Nairobi. It required careful driving to avoid the many deep potholes. An interesting ride, passing many small villages on the way when after an hour and a half we came to Mount Longonot, and a viewing area looking down from 8000ft into the Great Rift Valley. It really was a spectacular sight.

On the way back, the children asked if we could go into the Nairobi Wildlife Game Park. Sunset was not far away and of course being near the Equator when it happens, it happens fast, but Amin said OK. We entered the park, and drove quite away in before seeing any animals, but then Amin had to brake sharply to avoid two giraffes, which suddenly appeared on the path. More giraffes and gazelles were spotted and then we met another car whose driver told us that a little way further on, a lion had made a kill. Amin drove on, and indeed we had a good view of the lion, which was not at all interested in us thank goodness. Its supper was far more important!

By now the sun had set and darkness was falling rapidly, so Amin started to head for the exit. The problem was that he had criss-crossed several paths and had no idea which way to go. With headlights on, we seemed to drive around in circles for ages, and just as an element of panic was creeping in, we saw another vehicle ahead and followed that. Fortunately that car knew where it was going and we emerged from the Park, very relieved.

Kenya must be a fascinating country to explore, but it was time to move on.

Next stop, and my final one for this trip, was Blantyre in Malawi. A new snack food factory was being built with British equipment and we were tendering for the packaging material. I was beginning to realise just how big Africa is on the flight from Nairobi to Lilongwe the capital of Malawi, I had a superb view of Mount Kilimajaro, but then there seemed little to see from the air but the plains below. At Lilongwe I had to transfer to the domestic flight to Blantyre, and it was on this flight that I had my worst experience of flying.

Blantyre is approximately two hundred miles south of Lilongwe and I was travelling on an old Air Malawi BAC 1-11 jet. The flight would be the best part of one hour and we climbed to a fair height after take off. After the seat belt sign had eventually been switched off, a stewardess started to come from the back of the plane with a drink's trolley. She was about a third of the way down the aisle when the aircraft suddenly went into a steep dive. Fortunately I still had my seat belt fastened but many passengers did not and I was aware of several being thrown forward against the seat in front. The trolley sped forward and hit the pilot's door scattering its contents into the air. Other loose articles were flying around. It was chaos. Then just as suddenly, the aircraft levelled out and soon we were landing at Blantyre. The odd thing was that it was not until I had left the aircraft that I felt any emotion at all, and that was pure relief. The speed of events on board, were such that I don't think there was time to feel scared.

The reason we were given for the rapid descent was that the aircraft had lost pressure suddenly and the pilot needed to reduce height to a couple of thousand feet.

My meeting with the company in Blantyre was not successful. Although our offer was competitive, it was not enough to obtain an order, which went to a South African company. It was easier to import from there than the UK.

From my brief two day visit I could see that Malawi is a beautiful country, but there was no time to explore. I was not looking forward to the return trip to Lilongwe. We were told that the BAC 1-11 had been grounded and that we would be making the journey on an even older plane, a turboprop Hawker Siddley HS 748 – 50 seater. This had been in service since 1969. After take off, it lumbered on at not a great height taking about one and a half hours to reach Lilongwe. Not an experience I want to repeat.

So at the end of my search for new markets, the results were mixed to say the least, but that was life in the export world. In January 1991, we would start the exercise all over again.

Chapter 26

Tis neither here nor there

OTHELLO WILLIAM SHAKESPEARE

1990 was proving to be what you might call a challenging year. To help our associate companies in Holland, France, Spain and Greece we had linked them up with a major export account each and persuaded them to deal direct thus freeing us up to find other markets. In addition we had handed responsibility for the Caribbean area to our Dutch company. They had appointed an agency consisting of two Dutch brothers to travel to the area and seek out business. This arrangement had been going on for quite a long period but then problems occurred. Payments, which should have been transferred to our Dutch company, were not handed over and were being pocketed by the agency. Legal action then took place and the agency was terminated.

We were asked to help by finding agents in Trinidad, Barbados, Jamaica and Guyana. Notices were posted in the bulletins issued by the various commercial sections of the British Embassies or Consulates in each country, and we received responses from each. So it was now a question of who should go and get things sorted.

By November it was clear that Saddam's occupation of Kuwait was going to be short lived. The Arab League were united against him, and following a UN resolution, forces were being assembled in Saudi Arabia ready for a full scale attack early in 1991.

Meanwhile in the UK, the political scene was in turmoil. The popularity of Mrs Thatcher's government had sunk to an all time low and there were rumblings of discontent from even her most devoted supporters. The economy was once again on the decline and there was already talk of the dreaded word "recession". The pressure therefore was to get as much export business as possible. The other full-time export rep. was busy scouring central and west Africa whilst our clerical assistant, who did a great job for both of us, was given his chance to travel and went to Norway and Poland.

That left me. I did manage a short September trip to Cairo and Khartoum but in the circumstances, making my usual trip to Saudi Arabia in November was not considered practical because of the Iraq situation. So, lucky me drew the short straw to go to the Caribbean. There was no shortage of volunteers to carry my bags!

This was a 12-day trip to Barbados, Trinidad and Guyana. It was decided to leave Jamaica for the time being.

Barbados was first stop. It is undoubtedly a beautiful island, and a playground for the well off. As I headed out of the hotel reception to meet one of the agency applicants, all the other guests were heading out of the opposite door for the beach! I won't ask for your sympathy!

The first company did not impress me but the second one seemed to have the right connections and knew the island's industries well. I was to find out quickly that inter island trade was as important as the tourist trade. What also struck me about Barbados was the fact that all the hotels and up market housing were situated on the right, along the coastline road, whilst poor quality dwellings and shacks were on the left hand side. It was a contrast that jarred on me, and I couldn't help comparing this with the standard of living I had seen in Mauritius.

After just two days it was off to Trinidad, which we had identified as being the major market in the area. I had allowed for a week here. Trinidad is certainly a working island and not a tourist destination. It is the neighbouring island of Tobago, which attracts the tourists and the more affluent folk from Trinidad at weekends. It was not on my itinerary.

Here I had a big stroke of luck. We had had only one enquiry about our agency from a man called Robert de Montbrun. He was a retired businessman who was forming an agency to serve the food production industry. He had been the managing director of the island's brewery and it became obvious during our first meeting that he was well acquainted with businesses in Trinidad and had many contacts. So I was delighted when he agreed to become our agent, and I promised our company's full support. During the week therefore, I was able, with Bob's help, to see many companies and obtain firm enquiries. Many companies relied upon exporting products to other islands, and in particular to the USA, so good quality packaging was essential.

I was intrigued by the de Montbrun name and wanted to find out more. Bob has given me some details of his family's history and it reads rather like one of those *Who Do You Think You Are* programmes, which have been so interesting on the BBC.

As the name suggests, the family originated in France and a de Montbrun was one of Napoleon's top Generals. However members of the family moved to Spain, and later in the 19th century sought a new life in Latin America, namely Venezuela. If you look at the map you will see that it is close to Trinidad, and it is here that they ended up. They were not land speculators like many of those who left Europe for the New World, but lawyers and doctors. Bob's father then emigrated to Canada in the 1920s where he met his wife. They had four children, two boys and two girls but the depression of the 1930s brought difficult times for the family and they moved back to Trinidad where the grandparents still lived.

Bob and his father started a food import business in 1958, which eventually grew into eight companies of which Bob was Chairman until he retired. Not one to let all that commercial experience go to waste, he then set up the Commission Agency which is today run by his grandson also named Robert.

Final stop was Georgetown in Guyana. This former colony, which was called British Guiana, had been up until now the poor relation of the area. Now exports of timber, demerara sugar, and minerals from the interior had provided the resources necessary to start modernising. This process was in its infancy at the time of my visit though.

When I checked in for my flight due at 5.30pm, there were few other passengers. The check-in lady asked me if I had booked transport at the other end because I would be arriving at 7.30pm, which was after dark. She told me that the airport was one hours drive from Georgetown and that there had been several recent incidents of robbery on the road after dark. "Just make sure you get a good taxi" was the advice. I wasn't too worried because the hotel, which I had booked, ran a mini bus service to and from the airport, so I hoped that it would be waiting to pick up passengers when I arrived.

It wasn't! Nor were there any obvious taxis around. After a short wait, a man drew up in a battered taxi and I got in and told him the name of my hotel. He then drove like the proverbial bat out of hell. The vehicle's suspension took a terrible battering on the road and we saw hardly any other cars but finally arrived at around 9pm. That evening I saw on the television in my room, that Mrs Thatcher had resigned.

The main street in Georgetown reminded me of one of those Hollywood "wild west" films. There was a wide street with wooden buildings on either side in a variety of architectural styles. We already had one good customer here who had remained loyal to us over many years but his offices were a throwback to the old colonial days I reckon, with dark brown office furniture everywhere.

I did appoint another agent, so after a couple of days my task was done, and it was time to get back to the UK. In order to give the new agencies the best possible start, I agreed to go back early in the New Year and left at the end of January. This time I included Jamaica.

I was keeping an eye on the situation in the Middle East. Operation "Desert Storm" to clear Saddam's forces out of Kuwait had commenced on January 17th 1991.

The ten day visit to Barbados, Trinidad, and Jamaica showed that things were going well in the first two. Bob had really got to grips with the business in Trinidad. He took me to lunch at a restaurant in Port of Spain, which was well used by the business community. We sat at a table on the first floor next to the stairs, which led to the dining room. I noticed that practically all the men that came up the stairs noticed Bob, and greetings were exchanged. It was a good sign.

Jamaica was somewhat different. My arrival at Kingston had not been exactly smooth. The airport is on a long strip of land, which stretches out to sea around Kingston harbour, eleven miles from the city. I took a taxi but, on nearing the city, it broke down on the main highway and I had to help the driver push it into the side of the road. He then flagged down another cab and I finally got to my hotel.

A visit to the one biscuit and confectionery manufacturer of any size, did not reveal any good prospects. They were buying some poor quality material from a local printer and were not looking to export. Kingston struck me as very run down, and there were warning signs in the hotel, recommending guests not to wander the streets especially at night.

The Gulf War ended on February 28th 1991, and I waited for an opportunity to get a visa to go to Saudi Arabia again. With Iraq and Kuwait now off the scene, it was vital to get as much as I could out of the industrial expansion that was going on inside the Kingdom. We had lost the Yemen business to competition, and I had heard that they were going to set up their own printing company.

It was May before I was finally able to organise the trip. I went to Dhahran on the May 14th just ten days after returning from a quick seven day visit to Trinidad. Things were starting to get complicated trying to keep everyone happy.

Dhahran was still feeling the effects of Saddam's firing of Kuwait's oil fields. The black smoke had drifted southwards and was clearly visible. Existing companies in all three sectors, Dhahran, Riyadh and Jeddah were now pushing ahead with new products, and I was getting information from good contacts about further new companies. I even found one new client waiting for me in the company car park in Bristol when I came to the office at 7.30am. He had come overnight from Jeddah, then driven to Bristol. He had brought some croissants from his bakery, and wanted photographs of them to appear on his packaging. I managed to find a photographer to oblige and the client returned home that night happy with the result.

Things calmed down a bit during the summer but there was still the need to service the Caribbean area again in

October. As well as Barbados, Trinidad and Guyana, I decided to go to Guatemala as well. For many years, we had received orders from two companies, and I found out that no one from our company had ever visited them. We had an agent there, who was also British Cellophane's agent. It was a Mrs Abbot.

The agency was started in the 1960s by Mr. Abbot, but sadly he had died a while ago. Mrs Abbot decided to keep the agency going and was being helped by her daughter Julie, who was studying at college to become an electrical engineer. Income from the agency was helping to pay the college fees.

A visa was required, which delayed things a little, but eventually I set off at the end of September. There was no direct flight, so I transited via Miami.

It was my first experience of Latin America, and I find it difficult to accurately describe Guatemala City, the capital. It is situated at 5000ft above sea level and with the high pollution, it can make breathing difficult. The city is divided into twenty two zones, but several of these zones were controlled by violent criminal gangs and the murder rate was running at fifty five a week. Uncomfortably near to the city are four volcanoes, two of which are active and occasionally spewed clouds of dust over the surrounding area. I was staying at the Camino Real Hotel, which conjures up visions of a "spaghetti western", but it was a good hotel. There were the same warnings to guests as existed in Jamaica about going out unaccompanied.

Julie came to collect me in a battered old pick-up truck. She said she never bothered to lock the vehicle. She just removed the steering wheel at night. Most of the other vehicles we saw were battered too, and would not have looked out of place in a stock car race. Mind you, being driven around was like being in a stock car event. Normal rules of the road did not apply, and it was just as well that Julie's truck was bigger than most of the other vehicles and she took no prisoners. *Top Gear* would like it here. We visited our two customers and were warmly received. On day two, we went to the outskirts of the city, where a plantation was growing flowers, exotic plants, and soft fruits, all of which were destined for the American market. One of our associate companies in Spain had developed a special container for the transportation of this type of product, so I took all the necessary information to pass on when I returned to the UK.

So after only two days, I left for Barbados, Guyana, and Trinidad getting back to the UK on the October 12th. I then needed to get visas and put together a trip to the Middle East before the end of the year.

All this coming and going, east/west/east/west was proving counter productive and I really felt as if I was losing my grip on the Middle East. I really wanted to focus on the markets I knew best. I put this to our MD and he agreed. It was decided to pass responsibility for the Caribbean to other members of commercial staff. There was no shortage of volunteers!

By February 1992, the UK was in its longest running recession since the end of the war. John Major was now Prime Minister facing huge problems. Unemployment had reached two and a half million, and was still rising. My colleagues and I were scouring all our export markets for business. I did four long trips, which included Saudi Arabia, Egypt, Sudan, Bahrain, Qatar, Dubai and Oman. The market was still holding up but competition was even greater than before. We were hanging on to our Sri Lankan business, just about, and top managers were taking turns to go to the Caribbean – to work, honest!

Things however were about to become even more complicated for me and the company requiring some careful decisions to be made.

Chapter 27

East, West, Home's Best
HG Bohn 1855

I have a vague memory in my childhood of an embroidered or cross-stitch picture hanging over the fireplace either in my great grandmother's house or that of some other elderly relative. It showed a pretty cottage surrounded by a garden full with colourful flowers. Above the house were the words "East, West, Home's Best".

I grew up at a time when foreign travel was only for the rich and famous. Many people never left their town or village in their entire life. If we were lucky then a once a year trip to the seaside was as near as we got to any sort of travel experience.

In saying that however I am forgetting that I was fortunate enough to get on a school trip to Switzerland in 1947. It cost £15 and we were allowed to take £3 pocket money. I was able to go simply because I had saved this amount from money given to me during the war years at birthdays and Christmas by my many aunts and uncles. My parents certainly could never have afforded the cost. The experience was an eye opener. Travelling by train, ferry and more trains, the journey took almost two days. However seeing a country untouched by war was unforgettable, and when I retraced my steps sixty years later in 2007 I knew that my memories were not exaggerated in any way.

There was a man in our village who, in 1949, entered the Monte Carlo Rally. News of this spread quickly around the village, and for a while he became quite a celebrity. Our next door neighbours owned one of the few cars in the village. They were quite well to do, and every year they went on holiday to St Ives in Cornwall, which to us then, was almost akin to a foreign destination. When our family moved to Bristol, it had the same impact on our friends in the north as it would today if someone went to live in Australia.

How the world has shrunk in the last fifty years. Travel is now part of everyday life, and is now available to all. In the relatively short time that I had been working, the UK had been opened up by the network of motorways, high speed trains, and flights to and from regional airports. I could catch a flight from Bristol to Glasgow at 7am, be at our factory there by 9am, catch the afternoon flight back to Bristol and be home in time for tea.

Whereas in 1974, when I did my first trip, finding connecting flights was difficult, by 1993 the network of the world's airlines made travelling almost as easy as catching a bus.

The mobile phone age was not far away. Communication technology has today reached a level, which frankly leaves me baffled. It amazes me that I can send a message and pictures to the other side of the world in seconds.

Back to 1974 and none of this modern equipment was available although no doubt clever people were working on it. I recall around that time a *Tomorrow's World* programme on the BBC showing grainy black and white pictures of a tram leaving its depot in Melbourne. The pictures had come via a new communication satellite in space. Now events from the remotest part of the world reach our screens in minutes.

So, into 1993 and servicing our markets had become

easier. Of course visas still had to be obtained but even here the waiting times had come down. The recession of 1992 had now passed its worst stage, and the economic position of the country was starting to look brighter. John Major was now an elected Prime Minister having won the general election in April 1992. In September 1992, the UK had withdrawn from the Exchange Rate Mechanism, which fixed the value of the pound against other currencies. The Pound was now allowed to find its own level particularly against the dollar and this had worked in favour of our exports.

Whilst the domestic market was still suffering the after effects of the recession even though inflation was down to 1%, the need to export was still as great as ever. In the first half of the year I had done two trips, criss-crossing the Middle East, and still getting good business especially as quite a lot of orders were paid for in dollars.

Many big companies had suffered in the 1992 recession and Courtaulds was no exception. It operated in three distinctly different fields, textiles, packaging, and industrial paint. The textile business had collapsed because of cheap imports from the Far East. Packaging was not giving adequate returns from all its European companies although our site was performing well.

However, investment in new machinery for our factory was due. Our major printing presses had been running for twenty four hours a day for ten years with only a ten day gap each year for servicing. Our competitors in the UK and Europe were installing state of the art equipment, and it was going to cost millions to bring in new machines.

Rumours abounded during the summer months, and finally we heard that Courtaulds were pulling out of packaging by the end of the year. Colodense was being sold to a Scottish company.

This was a totally new scenario for me, and for many other long serving employees. I had been here for forty years and many of my colleagues had also been here for over thirty years. The options put to us were fairly simple, stay on and work for the new company but the pension fund would be transferred, and would not be payable until reaching the retirement age of 65. The other option was to retire [I was 58] but at least I could do so and receive a pension of two thirds of my final salary. Having talked the matter over with my wife Ve, I opted for retirement but accepted a consultancy, which would see me working 90 days a year to assist my replacement whoever that might be.

Once the initial shock had worn off, I felt quite relieved. Travelling had become stressful. Three hour check in times, high security, and always the demand for work from our group companies, had put even more pressure on the export team. Nevertheless handing over the Middle East to someone else would be hard I knew. I had dealt with many of the companies for an awful long time, and had built up a good relationship with the owners.

Adverts were placed in the quality UK press. From the replies, a short list of three was drawn up, and I sat in on the interviews. Only one of the candidates seemed suitable but turned down the offer we made.

Take over by the Scottish company was due officially on the December 31st and by the time I had got back from my September trip, we were no nearer getting anyone to replace me. Then as sometimes happens in life, we had a bit of good fortune in that we heard from British Cellophane that one of their employees in South Africa was asking for a transfer back to the UK.

Bob, a family man, wife and two daughters, was based

in Johannesburg, and had become increasingly worried by the rising level of crime and violence in the area. He felt it was no longer the place for his family. He flew back for an interview and seemed perfect for the job. We were relieved when he accepted our offer and made plans to move back to the UK over the Christmas period.

Before that, I linked up with him in Bahrain at the end of November and took him around the whole region. Our customers were very welcoming and generous to me in their farewells.

Officially I retired on the December 31st 1993, and then was re-employed part time as from the January 1st 1994. The consultancy continued for three years mainly supporting Bob when he was travelling but further troubled times for the company continued with the company changing hands two more times, first to a Danish firm, and finally to an Australian group. The final twist was the transfer of production to Poland in 2006, a sad end for a well respected British company.

So what had I learnt from my time abroad. There is an old Arab saying that "one hand cannot clap by itself". There is no way I could have done what I did without the love and support of my wonderful wife, Ve, who dealt with my many absences superbly, looking after the family and the challenges that they brought. Also the full support of all my colleagues in Bristol, Glasgow and eventually contacts in our European companies. Then there were the people who ran our agencies to represent our company such as Moustafa in Iraq, Slaiman in Kuwait, Chandra in Sri Lanka, Bob in Trinidad, Julie in Guatemala, Jacques in Madagascar and Saad in London.

In the 1970s and 1980s, the feeling I got from all the countries I visited was that the UK was a fair and honest member of the UN and could be trusted. By the same token, rightly or wrongly, the USA was regarded as interfering and self-indulgent, always trying to impose its policies on all corners of the world. Today I fear that the UK has now become irrevocably linked with the USA, and our reputation for being even handed is tarnished. I wish it were possible to put up a sign in the Foreign Office saying that Britain does NOT have an Empire any more. I cringe when I hear some glib politician talk about "our national interest". I always insert the word "selfish" before "national" and see how the argument stands up then. Double standards exist where "our interests" aren't affected. Why aren't we bombing Syria, Yemen or Zimbabwe? No oil to worry about there. But enough of my rant!

With English being taught as the second language, it comes as no surprise that it is the UK and USA where many overseas students want to go to, to finish their studies. The UK's education system and healthcare provision is much admired. The problem for many developing countries was to attract their young people back once their education was complete. Too often they found better opportunities where they were.

This was particularly true in the Middle East countries that I worked in. I found parents actively encouraging their sons and daughters to remain in the UK or USA. The unsettled political scene that has existed over the decades in the Middle East shows no sign of calming down as events are now proving. Despite this, companies wanted to produce goods that would benefit and improve the life of ordinary people, provide work for their employees, and generally push the development of their country forward. It was not their fault that their efforts would be hampered by power hungry dictators, absolute monarchs, and extreme fundamentalism.

For my part, wherever I went, I was met with kindness and great hospitality. Life in the export world was always challenging and never dull. I hope that I have managed to convey something of this in my narrative and that you have enjoyed the trip. Time to fasten your seat belt for the final landing.

Thank you for your company. Come to think of it, the conversation has been very one sided! I hope you have not been bored with my tale.

As we part, I will leave you with one final thought. We are all imperfect beings in an imperfect world.

The rain it raineth on the just,
And also on the unjust fella:
But chiefly on the just, because
The unjust steals the just's umbrella

BARON BOWEN, 1835–1894

Farewell.

Acknowledgements

In writing this book I have used information from several sources:

This Sceptred Isle – Twentieth Century BBC/Penguin
The Arab World Gerald Butt, BBC
Worlds Apart Gavin Young, Penguin
Journey For A Soul George Appleton, Fontana
Good News Bible Collins
The World's Religions Lion Handbooks
Kabul to Kandahar Oxford University Press
Dictionary of Quotations D C Browning, Dent
Wikipedia
Donna and Slaiman Esh Shaya
Robert de Montbrun

Thanks also to our son Michael and good friend Joan Clark for their help in getting this book ready for publication.

Lightning Source UK Ltd.
Milton Keynes UK
UKOW052040100712

195760UK00001B/5/P